BUYING AND SELLING BUSINESSES

BUYING AND SELLING BUSINESSES

Including Forms, Formulas, and Industry Secrets

William W. Bumstead

Special Section on Valuing Businesses by
George D. Abraham

John Wiley & Sons, Inc.

New York • Chichester • Weinheim • Brisbane • Singapore • Toronto

Library of Congress Cataloging-in-Publication Data:

Bumstead, William W.
    Buying and selling businesses: including forms, formulas, and industry secrets / William W. Bumstead.
        p.   cm.
    Includes bibliographical references and index.
    ISBN 0-471-24336-1 (cloth : alk. paper)
    1. Sale of business enterprises—United States. 2. Corporations—Valuation—United States.   I. Title.
    HD1393.4.U686   1998
    658.1'—dc21   97-29025

Printed in the United States of America.
10 9 8 7 6 5 4 3 2 1

To
Mazzi
and
Victor
Wonderful Examples of
Kindness, Generosity and Unselfish Love

ABOUT THE AUTHOR

William W. Bumstead. In addition to assisting business owners and managers in the enhancement, performance, and value of businesses, Mr. Bumstead has spent over 25 years selling and training others to sell businesses and professional practices. His accomplishments have included two college degrees, a Series 7 NASD Securities License, and a Texas Securities License. He has received a real estate broker license in Colorado and Texas and achieved the status of Broker of the Year of the Texas Association of Business Brokers.

Mr. Bumstead served as president of the Houston, Texas, Chapter of the Texas Association of Business Brokers and state president of the Texas Association of Business Brokers. He was a member of board of directors of the Houston, Texas, Chapter of the Texas Association of Business Brokers for three years and a member of state board of directors of the Texas Association of Business Brokers for four years. He is also a fellow of the International Business Brokers Association. His professional certifications include: Certified Business Counselor of the Institute of Certified Business Counselors (CBC), Certified Business Intermediary (Fellow) of the International Business Brokers Association (FCBI), Board

ABOUT THE AUTHOR

Certified Broker of the Texas Association of Business Brokers (BCB), Professional Business Consultant of the Alliance of Business Consultants (ABC), and Licensed Private Investigator (LPI), State of Texas.

Author of books, professional training manuals, and articles in state and national professional journals, Mr. Bumstead is also a very successful speaker and trainer. Residing in Colordo with his wife Mari, he is an active business consultant, with a personal inventory of businesses for sale.

ABOUT THE CONTRIBUTOR

George D. Abraham has been involved in the transfer of over 450 businesses in the past 20 years. His company was the first in the nation to develop and gain national attention for its unique and highly accurate business evaluation software programs which are marketed by John Wiley & Sons, Inc., worldwide and used in nearly 1,400 offices.

Mr. Abraham is a licensed Real Estate Broker, Real Estate Appraiser, Business Appraiser, Machinery and Equipment Appraiser, Board Certified Business Broker, Certified Environmental Inspector, Certified Business Intermediary, licensed State Property Tax Consultant, Accredited Review Appraiser, Certified Business Counselor, and prior instructor for the Continuing Education Real Estate Course in Business Appraisal at the University of Houston. He is retained regularly by attorneys, accountants, and other clients for appraisals, as well as court testimony as an expert witness.

Currently on the National Board of Directors for the Institute of Certified Business Counselors and serving as the national vice president of Education, Mr. Abraham also writes articles for association newsletters and speaks at national conventions for this industry. He has conducted over 34 seminars on business valuation in the United States and Canada and was listed as one of the top appraisers in 1993 in *Turnarounds & Workouts* news publication.

DISCLAIMER BY THE AUTHOR

The purchaser and practitioner of the information contained herein should understand that the ideas, calculations, examples, and projections of accomplishments in these pages and classroom sessions must not be construed as guaranteed, normal, or achievable and that the generic forms, files, and materials are presented for study, classroom discussion, and demonstration purposes only. You are hereby notified not to copy or use any form printed herein.

You should acknowledge that your personal achievements will be determined by your own objectives and efforts and are not the responsibility of the author, publisher, or any of their representatives. You must be responsible for your personal compliance with the city, county, state, and federal laws and regulations regarding professional services you offer to the public. You should check with the local Intermediary Associations, as well as the Board of Realtors, Real Estate Commission, Securities Commission(s), Attorney General's Office, and/or your own attorney regarding the requirements of all forms, agreements, procedures, laws, regulations, and Deceptive Trade Practices Act, the Unauthorized Practice of Law, and licensing for which you may be responsible. The author and publisher assume no responsibility for your compliance with any of the above! Your purchase of these materials and agreement to participate in any classroom activities is with the understanding that neither the author nor publisher is engaged in rendering legal advice and cannot guarantee in any way the proper and correct use of the information provided.

If you have a question about anything, for your own protection, do your research.

We live in an ever increasing litigious society. You need to adequately prepare yourself for a nonlitigious career!

Congratulations for your entrepreneurial foresight to enter and/or improve your participation in this industry. Your efforts should produce dividends for many years!

William W. (Bill) Bumstead
CBC, FCBI, BCB, LREB, PBC, LPI

CONTENTS

CONTENTS

ACKNOWLEDGMENTS

When others spend their hard earned money attending my seminars and reading my materials I feel a genuine responsibility to share with them more than just my own inbred ideas. This is why I have enlisted some of the most respected professionals in our industry to review these pages prior to their publication.

Even though we all spend a lot of time sharing at conventions and conferences, I still find myself operating too much in my own little world. Their comments are sincerely appreciated! I respect their opinions and the readers will be better served by their observations.

I am very grateful to Mr. George D. Abraham, owner of Business Evaluation Systems, for his contribution of Chapter 1.

I am indebted to the following, and many others through the years, for their willingness to share from their wealth of experience:

Bob Gurrola, FCBI, CBC, LREB
President, International Business Brokers Association

Wally Stabbert, CBC
President, The Institute of Certified Business Counselors

ACKNOWLEDGMENTS

Tom West, FCBI, LREB
Business Brokerage Press

Bob Evans, CBI, CBC, LREB
President, Texas Association of Business Brokers

Don McIver, CBI, BCB, LREB
American Business Group, Inc.

Brian Knight, FCBI, LREB
Country Business, Inc.

Lyn Crader, CBC, LREB
Tamra Newby (Crader)
Crader & Associates, Inc.

Bill Womack, FCBI, BCB, LREB
Connie Womack, FCBI, BCB, LREB
Landmark Business Brokers

Mary Jane Dailey, FCBI, BCB, LREB
Ron Payton, CBI, BCB
Dailey Resources, Inc.

Ernie Bruss, CBC, LREB
BIZOPS

Eldon Edwards, FCBI, LREB
Inco Business Sales

Ed Hart, CBC, FCBI, BCB, LREB
Shirley Hart
International Business Exchange Corporation

William Erik Bumstead, LPI, PBI
Worldwide Claim Services, Inc.

Mari Bumstead, BBA, LREB

Gary Cooper, CPA

James Sawyer, CPA, BCB, LREB

Jeffrey A. Lehmann
Attorney

Peter Nemkov
Attorney

Richard Melamed
Attorney

INTRODUCTION

These Pages Should Be Required Reading for Every Business Seller, Potential Business Buyer, and the Professionals Who Assist Them in Buying, Selling, and Valuing Privately Held Businesses!

At some point every business owner will exit his/her business for which there will be potential buyers. The earlier they begin preparations for this event, the more rewarding the experience should be for all concerned! This volume is written to assist in a better understanding between business sellers and buyers as well as an improved performance of the professionals they engage in the process of buying, selling, and valuing businesses. Removing the guesswork and revealing the secrets of success to all parties involved will improve working relationships and produce more successful transactions. Business buyers and sellers will gain a better understanding of how intermediaries, accountants, attorneys, and other counselors can assist them in their deal making. These professionals will find proven ideas to dramatically improve their efficiency.

INTRODUCTION

A BRIEF HISTORY

Buying, selling, and valuing businesses as an industry has become more widely recognized in the last 50 years. It is encouraging to know the transfer of business ownership has been practiced since the beginning of recorded history with some references even recorded in the Book of Ruth in the Bible.

Intermediaries, who were previously called business transfer agents, are reported to have been handling business sales in Europe over 250 years ago. In America, advertisements of business broker services have been traced in publications to the 1920s. In the 1960s a few chains offering business broker services began to emerge in the United States and by the 1970s we saw some business brokerage franchises spread across the country. Professionals involved in this trade have been found in yellow page advertisements in all states, Washington, DC, Puerto Rico, Brazil, Canada, England, Spain, Sweden, Switzerland, and several other countries around the world.

PROFESSIONALS SERVING BUYERS AND SELLERS OF BUSINESSES

Some have estimated there are currently between 1,500 and 2,000 firms in the United States whose only or main objective is the offering of intermediary services to buyers and sellers of businesses. An aggressive guess is that there are a total of 10,000 professionals working in these offices. Most of these firms are small, however some have 10, 20, and more agents in their offices. Some of the 1 million or so licensed real estate agents in the United States offer business intermediary services. Other professionals involved in business valuations and sales are attorneys, accountants, merger and acquisition specialists, investment bankers, venture capitalists, stockbrokers, business counselors, business valuators/ appraisers, and so on.

Because of the inconsistency of formal transaction recording practices in most states, it is difficult to ascertain the true dollar volume of business sales transactions in the United States. Some have estimated it to be in excess of $400 billion annually. One thing for sure, we are currently enjoying some of the best years.

PROFESSIONAL TRADE ASSOCIATIONS

The organization of professionals in the industry has grown in maturity as well as in numbers with the forming of state trade associations, such as the Texas Association of Business Brokers (TABB) in Houston, Texas, in 1978. Others now exist in several states. Later, in 1983, some of those instrumental in founding the Texas Association of Business Brokers also participated in the initiation of the International Business Brokers Association (IBBA), now the largest in the industry. The Institute of Certified Business Counselors (CBC) may well be one of the oldest trade associations which includes a healthy mix of all professionals involved in counseling, valuing, accounting, brokering, financing, and legal services.

TERMINOLOGY

One area with which the industry continues to struggle is the lack of consistency in terminology. Some of the trade associations are making significant efforts to agree on common terms, however the results are slow in coming, which leaves the public confused. For instance, is the professional who assists a business owner in the sale of a business an intermediary, a business transfer agent, a business broker, a mergers and acquisitions specialist, a business counselor, or what? Is the person who wants to sell a business a seller or a divestor? Is the person buying a business a buyer or an investor? Is the cash flow that remains after business expenses are paid called discretionary cash flow, net profit, cash flow before taxes, cash flow after taxes, earnings before interest and taxes, earnings before interest depreciation and taxes, earnings before interest depreciation, taxes, and amortization, or any one of several other widely used terms?

GENERAL ECONOMIC CLASSIFICATIONS

Another confusing issue is the classification of businesses by economic size. I have seen some try to accomplish this by using these categories:

1. Privately held smaller businesses (usually under $500,000 sales price) which comprise approximately 3/4 of the total.

2. Privately held larger businesses (usually priced from $500,000 to $1,000,000 and up in sales price).

3. Publicly held companies (ranging from $1,000,000 to $20,000,000 and up in sales price).

4. Publicly held companies (ranging from $20,000,000 and up in sales price).

Practically, from a marketing standpoint, some have classified them into categories based on the anticipation of where and how the buyers may be found.

1. Privately held businesses with buyers most logically to be found in a local or regional asset sale marketing effort.
2. Privately held businesses with buyers most logically to be found in a national/international asset sale marketing effort.
3. Publicly held companies.

The answers to these terminology conflicts will someday be a complete published volume, and hopefully available soon. We will deal with some of the terminology in the Glossary section at the back of the book.

FORMS OF OWNERSHIP

Even though there may be small variances from state to state, we find more agreement in the common terms in different forms of ownership, such as:

- Sole proprietorships
- "C" corporations
- Closed corporations
- "S" corporations
- Limited liability companies
- General partnerships

- Professional or personal service partnerships
- Family partnerships
- Joint ventures

BUSINESS TYPE CLASSIFICATIONS

Regarding different types of businesses, the potentially most confusing issue in our industry has been made the most simple to understand by the federal government with the publication of the *Standard Industrial Classification Manual* by the Office of Management and Budget (OMB) of the Executive Office of the President of the United States. This book contains almost 19,000 different business classifications which are given specific numerical identifications and placed in almost 100 major groups under 11 divisions. Most professionals and principals active in buying, selling, and valuing businesses use this information (SIC Codes) to identify the specific type of business. If you do not already own this manual, it should be your next purchase! Please refer to the Industry Resource List in this book.

An important issue may well be the determination of an asset or stock sale. This issue will be covered in subsequent chapters because there are several factors for your consideration.

REMOVING THE GUESSWORK

Welcome to our effort at taking the guesswork out of buying, selling, and valuing businesses. Mr. George D. Abraham is a master at determining the proper price for a business and has written Chapter 1, Valuing Businesses. Instead of the too-often found trial-and-error intermediary skills, you will find more professional ways to become a conscientious negotiator, painstakingly meticulous in the punctual handling of every detail. Confidentiality is another key to success you will acquire as you understand how to whisper in the right ears instead of yelling at the world.

The secrets of success of owners, buyers, sellers, intermediaries, and other professionals serving the industry may well be the best kept secret in town. Learning these necessary skills is an educational process from which you will never graduate. You will become more efficient, fast, and still genuinely attentive to every detail involved in a transaction. A person's business is his/her life and professionals will learn how to participate with each of them like a member of their own family. This volume will be one of many that will bring you benefits from the industry. It is not a technical presentation, but rather a practical approach to help professionals achieve a greater degree of success. Owners, buyers, and sellers of businesses will learn more about one of the most important steps in their lives and increase their understanding of how to better interact with professionals they engage in buying, selling, and owning businesses.

To my knowledge, there are no university degrees or other accolades of higher learning available in this specific field. Yet, there are educational opportunities provided by trade associations on a regular basis all across the United States, with hundreds of business owners, buyers, sellers, and the professionals they engage taking advantage of every opportunity to improve their skills and success. We don't study for degrees, we study in search of success. Welcome to one of these opportunities!

WE STUDY IN SEARCH OF SUCCESS

From Great Ranchers

"You can't come in contact
with anyone who can't
teach you something
you do not know."

Watt Matthews, Texas Rancher

To Multi-Million Dollar Industrialists

"If there is one secret to success,
it lies in the ability to
get the other person's point of view
and see things from his/her angle
as well as your own."

Henry Ford, Industrialist

Most Successful People

"Are open to new ideas,
ask many questions and
know how to listen!
They know that most of what they are
is a product of what
they have learned from others.
Successful people make the effort to
get outside of themselves to see
what others have to offer."

Adapted

Learn From Others!

"Take what you need
and give your best.
We study in search of success,
which is the real test!"

1

VALUING BUSINESSES

George D. Abraham
CBC, BCBA, AAR, FCBI, SPTC, RPM, CEI

INTRODUCTION

In selling businesses we all know the price is determined by what a reasonable buyer will pay a reasonable seller to buy his/her business.

Unfortunately to find a reasonable buyer to set that price is too expensive and time consuming. So, in the interest of setting a value, the art of appraisal was created to determine a value based on logical assumptions supported by evidence and documentation. Appraisers and brokers discovered over time that buyers generally tend to follow similar patterns of analysis.

Perhaps an insight into land and building appraisal, our sister industry, will explain some of the intrinsic problems of business appraisers. For example, land and buildings are generally appraised by historical sales records and those previous values are tempered with judgments about the economy and what a reasonable buyer will probably see as the future usefulness.

However, unlike home and land sales, there is no public recording of small business sales prices or what was actually exchanged. What makes evaluating a business more complicated is that intrinsic value is only in the assets that are owned or controlled by the business. Beyond that base, asset value is the value of profitability. Bankruptcy takes no skill; profitability takes knowledge, training, and time. Business value is a combination of profitability, security of those profits, and the transferability of operation methods.

Because historical business sales records are generally not available, many industries created their own *rules of thumb*. These methods were generally designed around historical records and tried to account for all the variables, but in the interest of simplicity, were created under the assumption of *other things being equal*. Every business owner knows that assumptions cause more problems and errors than any other single factor. The most common formulas created by any industry use a *gross multiplier*. The assumption is that a number times your gross sales is expected to yield a value of what you could reasonably expect to pay, *other things being equal*. No account was given to technological changes, consumer demand, or profitability, thus the *net multiplier* was created. This used net profit times a number to suggest a value; unfortunately, most companies try to minimize their tax cost thereby creating a false sense of net profit. Obviously these formulas assume too much to be truly representative, but they do have a place in the valuation process if tempered with additional data.

Until now the most comprehensive evaluation models were the most mathematically complex. With the advent of the computer for general business use, these models can now be calculated in the form of a professional evaluation at a cost of hours rather than weeks.

THE GROWING NEED FOR BUSINESS VALUATION

Over the last decade it has become apparent that businesses, like any other assets, need to be valued. In the past, very few individuals, both in the professional and business community, realized that a business was worth more than its book value. Over time those that recognized this added *intangible value* to the book value of a company were finally heard and the courts began to listen.

Although this chapter is mainly intended to address valuation for buying and selling businesses, it is important to at least make the reader aware of the many other reasons that businesses need to be valued. It also shows why business valuation will continue to grow.

1. Gift, estate, and inheritance taxes and estate planning.
    (a) Gift, estate, and inheritance taxes
    (b) Planning a program of family gifts
    (c) Recapitalization as a business and estate planning tool
    (d) Charitable contributions
2. Fair and enforceable buy-sell agreements between partners/shareholders.
3. Determining adequacy of life insurance.
    (a) For payment of taxes
    (b) Liquidation of estate stock
    (c) Continuity of business

4. Buying or selling shares in the company.

   (a) Estate and trust cases

   (b) Transactions with employees

   (c) Transactions with other shareholders

5. Employee stock ownership plans (ESOPs).

6. Corporate or partnership dissolutions.

7. Divorces.

8. Going public.

9. Going private.

10. Mergers.

   (a) Squeeze-out mergers—requires more than majority vote

   (b) Dissenters rights—protest compensation

11. Selling out.

12. Selling part interest or division of a company.

13. Making an acquisition.

14. Compensatory damage cases.

   (a) Breach of contract—lost business interest

   (b) Antitrust violations resulting in someone being forced out of business

   (c) Loss of business opportunity

   (d) Condemnation

15. Obtaining financing.

16. Reorganization under bankruptcy.

17. Allocation of total value.

   (a) Among classes of stock

   (b) Among classes of assets

18. Valuing trust or portfolio holdings.

19. Considering alternatives.

BUSINESS VALUATION—IS IT REALLY NECESSARY TO SELL A BUSINESS?

In talking to business brokers around the country, I have found myriad opinions ranging from a definite yes to an absolute defiance on the necessity of business valuation in the process of selling a business.

Several philosophies, however, stand out very strong. Some brokers feel that if you have been around awhile and know what you are doing, then a quick analysis of the company will tell you what it's worth. There is no doubt that there is some truth to this statement, but let's look a little deeper.

It is true that most good business brokers can quickly establish a fair asking price for the business without an extensive appraisal. The problem is that the seller usually wants twice as much for the business than what the broker has explained is fair market. Again, unlike the real estate industry, whereby value can be established by available similar historical comparable sales, usually in a specific area close to the subject, the business broker or business owner does not have that luxury.

This enables the real estate broker to easily prove what other similar properties in the area have sold for, thus the seller can quickly be educated as to a reasonable value. Both buyer and seller as well as their advisors in the deal can understand the value. This is especially important if outside financing is involved.

There is no recording of business sales and sellers have heard all kinds of inflated values. There is no quick way for the business broker to convince the seller that his price is too high. In most cases if the owner is serious about selling, he or she and the broker can agree on a value of the tangible assets, but it is the intangible assets that are in question and in most cases are more valuable than the tangible assets. Sellers invariably feel that the broker is trying to price the business too low so that he can sell it quickly and make the commission. Most serious sellers would be reasonable on price if they knew what was reasonable.

Somewhere in the negotiation on value each side will compromise. The seller agrees to a value close to what the broker feels is market value and the broker agrees to market the business for a higher price to cover the commission. The seller soon forgets what the broker said was fair market. He now has this new higher value firmly implanted in his mind.

Based on this price, he has established what he will clear, in cash, at closing. It is only natural for a buyer to question how the asking price was arrived at on the business. When he is told that it was based on what the broker and seller felt was fair market, and that was the extent of the valuation, then the buyer feels that the price is not really set, but only a starting point. Buyers are usually smart enough to know that in this type of valuation scenario the commission was added to a value that left room to negotiate. Since no formal method of pricing the business was used, the buyer feels that he should question the price. Buyers will also make much lower offers in order to test the seller concerning the bottom line. This upsets most sellers and they feel the buyer is either too stupid to run the business or is a thief. This is usually a difficult way to start negotiations and a tremendous amount of time is spent negotiating the price.

In most cases when a broker presents a decent offer to the seller it is usually much lower than he wants. Again, keep in mind that the seller has now convinced himself that the asking price is what he will get. The broker tries to convince the seller that the offer is indeed a good one since it is close to what he said it was worth in the first place. At this point the seller starts to feel that the broker is on the buyer's side and is attempting to make a quick deal in order to get his commission. The seller feels the broker is not even willing to try to negotiate a higher price.

The seller has seen the broker spend time and advertising dollars to market the business and is convinced that the broker really does feel like the asking price is justified. Why would he spend the time and money if he did not believe he could get that price? He feels betrayed by the broker and is upset that he is not receiving the net from the deal that he had counted on. Assuming he accepts the offer anyway, his attorney and accountant are now called in and the first question is how did you arrive at the price. The seller explains that the broker valued the business, but is not sure how he arrived at the value. Most attorneys and accountants at this time would question the price since it was set by an individual that will receive a commission much higher than the standard real estate commission they are accustomed to seeing. There are very few attorneys and accountants that are trained in business sales and valuation and the likelihood of the seller finding one is small. The same is true for the buyer and his advisors.

A good attorney and accountant are trained to protect their client's interest and the logical step at this point is to determine if the price is fair for their client. No wonder so many attorneys and accountants seem like deal killers and try their hand at business evaluation. If I were the attorney or accountant, I would try to educate myself about some formulas for pricing businesses to find out if my client was getting a fair deal. The most logical place for an attorney, banker, or an accountant to find pricing methods is from other friends or clients associated with the industry in question.

Most of these individuals have heard all sorts of industry

rules of thumb methods. These rules of thumb methods are usually a combination of net profit and assets or a multiple of net profit or even a multiple of gross sales. The problem is that there is no definition of net profit, assets, or sales given with the method. The accountant says that he has checked around and found that this type of company should sell for 6 to 10 times net plus the assets. Which net profit are you talking about: operating net, after tax, before tax, or net profit before interest and taxes? What about the assets: did they include real estate, was it a corporate sale, or an asset sale? Things can get out of hand very quickly and it appears that the broker is trying to push a deal through to get his commission and not really representing his client.

I have found that when I present the seller's attorney with an appraisal on the company, completed and paid for prior to the owner listing the business, this problem does not arise. When the buyer or his advisors question the asking price, the seller, if he chooses, has an excellent report to lend credence to his price. I also get referrals from the attorneys, accountants, and bankers because of the professional way I handled their client. The formal valuation report does not keep the buyer from negotiating, but it certainly narrows the range. It convinces the buyer that the seller has a valid reason for the asking price and anything too low will cause problems in negotiating.

Probably the strongest philosophy on this subject, if it is necessary to value a business in order to sell, is that the business broker does not need any extra liability. But one must also question if there is equal or greater liability for not doing an appraisal. I have found that no matter how the value was determined, should one party feel that they paid too much, or sold for too little, it was always the broker that had advised them of what it was worth. Each will claim that they relied on the broker's professional advice. Sellers enjoy telling other sellers, especially if they were competitors, what their businesses sold for. This will always be the actual price plus all future lease payments with options, plus all interest on notes plus 50% for good measure. Also don't forget the rules of thumb. If the sellers do not actually state the price they will always inflate the number of multiples for the rules of thumb methods.

Should, after the sale, an owner decide that he has sold too low, then the broker is the obvious villain. If there is no paper trail to explain how he determined the value, it leaves the broker with only a verbal explanation. A good attorney in a court of law will only ask questions that are answered with a yes or no. Those questions always seem out of context and the right answer sounds like the wrong answer. Most judges and juries are familiar with commissions on real estate but not on the sale of a business, so the fees can seem excessive. It is usually hard to convince a judge and jury that you did not serve your own best interest in establishing the price with yes or no statements.

I believe that if the broker had been paid to do an appraisal on the company prior to his taking the listing, then his day in court would be more convincing. At least he would have a written report that explained his methodology in reaching his conclusion of value. This would have to look more professional and ethical than verbal advice at the time the listing was taken. I am assuming the broker knows what he is doing, has done his appraisal report correctly, and his conclusions are supportable.

Another philosophy is that it is best not to even market the business with a price. This has been used mainly to market larger businesses and the idea is filtering down to smaller sales. The thinking is that this is the true method of finding out what the business is worth since the market itself does the valuation. A sophisticated buyer will and should do an analysis of the company's worth anyway, so why bother with the valuation for the seller? Who knows, the buyer may pay more for the business for a synergistic reason or may be using a rule of thumb method that is advantageous to the seller? I do not disagree, except that if the seller does not employ someone to tell him what the true fair market value of his company really is, then how will he know how to gauge the offers? If I were a seller, I doubt I would rely on valuation methods by the buyer.

Our industry is one of education. Each party to the transaction must feel they made a good deal. If the buyer feels he has made a good deal, but the seller is unsure, problems occur. Most sellers only see the good aspects of their business which is usually the reason he values his business too high. A good appraisal on the company will show the strengths and weaknesses of the company. Understanding some of the weaknesses of the company helps put the value in perspective for the seller. These weaknesses can become a positive for the buyer if he can correct them, thus enabling him to make the company more profitable.

To survive and prosper, a brokerage company must build a reputation that insures a constant flow of referrals. A growing number of brokerage companies will tell you that they are better known to the professional community as appraisers than as business brokers. Because of negative articles written about business brokerage in the last couple of years, attorneys, bankers, and accountants are somewhat reluctant to give referrals to business brokers. Most have no problem with referring their clients to an appraiser to find out what the business is worth. Then they discuss the tax and legal consequences. Once this has been accomplished, they can choose the business broker of their choice. If you have done a good appraisal and the seller decides to sell, very seldom will he go to another broker to sell the company. You are also ahead of the game when the seller is not only educated on value, but has analyzed and understands his tax and legal consequences before securing a buyer.

In summary, there is one area that we can all agree on. Time is money. Time spent by the broker on a business that does not sell is the same as an accountant whose client does not pay. Very few accountants could stay in business if only half their clients paid. The worst part is that while spending the time doing the books for the client that does not pay, the accountant has not had the time to secure new clients to make his business grow. The business broker's situation is no different. The seller that expects you to value, package, and market his business as part of your commission is the same as a company expecting to pay an accountant on a percentage of their income tax refund. Very few accountants could afford to do the tax work up front before determining if they should take on the client. In many cases, the very seller that won't pay for an appraisal on his company will usually spend twice the amount in legal and accounting fees proving to a buyer that an appraisal was not necessary in the first place.

The decade of the '80s brought a new type of buyer, one more sophisticated and informed. The personal computer gave the buyer and his advisors the means to crunch numbers in ways that before were only available to the very large corporations. We will find in the near future that we no longer will be able to market a business without a thorough analysis for our own protection. We will be charged, like any other professional, with making sure that the business we are representing is as it should be and that all information is supportable. In order to perform this duty, we will be forced to charge for our time if we are to be profitable. We will find, like other professionals who have grown past the stage of providing free information, that the client has more confidence in a professional that he pays.

TYPES OF VALUATION REPORTS

1. Oral report.

    This is obvious, except that it should be backed up with the proper calculations and research (to be discussed later in this report) and is simply stated to the owner. I have even seen this in court cases. The idea is that if you do not have a written report the opposing side has nothing to attack. However, I have not seen this tactic work well and it usually irritates the court.

2. Written reports.

    (a) Informal written report (letter of opinion).

         This is usually the same procedure as the oral report except that the appraiser only submits a letter stating the value. Both the oral report and the letter of opinion are a waste of time for all parties as they usually accomplish nothing. According to the Uniform Standards of Professional Appraisal Practice (USPAP), the main thrust of the standards is to insure that the average layperson should be able to follow the methodology and calculations and arrive at the same conclusion as the appraiser.

    (b) Summary report (range of value).

         The summary report (sometimes referred to as an evaluation) shows a range of values that the seller may receive in the way of offers on the company if put on the market. The appraiser in this case goes through all of the steps to a full appraisal, but since the report is usually not for court and is going to be presented for the owner's consideration, the appraiser may deviate from the USPAP by way of the departure provision. The departure provision is a simple statement that describes how and why the appraiser departed from the standards.

In most cases the summary report is well suited for sellers, buyers, and other individuals that are familiar with the industry and do not need to have a full written report describing the national, regional, and local economy, nor do they need a full write-up on the history and operations of the company and the industry outlook. Although these aspects are researched by the appraiser, he or she does not have to charge the client for unnecessary hours of writing. The other aspect of a summary report or an evaluation is that it shows the high and low ranges that would make sense for purchasing the company. These ranges represent various values that take into account synergism, terms and conditions, and many other factors that will be discussed later in this chapter. It also represents a value that may increase or decrease according to certain items on the balance sheet such as inventory levels, accounts receivable, accounts payable, cash on hand, as well as many other items that are changing on a day-to-day basis in the business.

(c) The formal report.

The formal report (or sometimes known as a full narrative report) is an appraisal that meets all of the provisions as set forth by the USPAP. The difference, other than a narrative on the business history and operations, industry outlook, local, regional, and national research, is that the formal report is *the value of a company on a specific date*. This type of report is usually the standard for values involving litigation or financing.

COMMON ERRORS IN APPRAISALS

In any type of appraisal it is imperative for the appraiser to understand the purpose and the function of the appraisal. In other words, what is the reason for the appraisal and what type of value is to be determined? This is where a good understanding of the clients' needs are critical.

Recently, I was asked to perform an appraisal of machinery, equipment, and real estate on a large industrial business to be used in conjunction with an overall business valuation for estate purposes. The major stockholder died and the son was to settle the estate. After my initial on-site inspection of the company the owner asked if I would contact the individual that was performing the business appraisal. He explained that the business appraiser wanted to interview the other appraisers and would have the final word as to who would be awarded the machinery, equipment, and real estate appraisal assignments.

When I contacted the business appraiser, he explained that he wanted a two-page report on the value of the machinery and equipment and the same for the real estate to be used in his appraisal. Because this was an oil field fabrication company, I asked him if they were profitable and his answer was that they were not. He agreed with me that the value would be mainly the assets that I was to value, but he still wanted a two-page report because they didn't want to spend a fortune on the appraisals. I explained that the cost was not that different, since you still had to do all the research and the only difference was that the report would not be printed. He still did not want a full report.

My quote was on a full report anyway and I basically told him I would give him a two-page report referencing the full report. I could only assume that the business appraiser wanted me to do a short form appraisal so that my fee would not interfere with his. The problem I had with this, other than the obvious, is that the value of the company would be the value of the machinery, equipment, and real estate and this therefore would not be a full report. This would surely be reason for IRS scrutiny. The first thing the owner had told me was the reason for the valuation was to try to eliminate problems with the IRS. In my mind, this type of report was sure to cause problems with the IRS. Unfortunately, because the appraiser was an old friend of the family and the owners had complete faith in him, I lost the assignment.

The point that I am trying to make is that a good appraiser must review the whole assignment and advise the client what is in his best interest. In this case, a full narrative report on the real estate and equipment was in the best interest of the client to accomplish his goals (not being contested by the IRS).

Another common error, amazingly, is failure to identify and conform to the applicable standard of value. In some cases this is merely an omission from the written report. In other cases, it may become apparent, from reading the report or questioning the appraiser, that the appraiser has gone off to do an appraisal without ever determining the applicable standard of value. In some cases, the applicable standard of value is identified but apparently not understood, because the analysis and conclusions do not conform to the standard of value, or fail to address some of the factors implied in the value. Many times I have seen companies use some of the large auction companies to value their equipment. They were under the impression that this was the same as fair market value.

Apart from good logic and ethics, I have seen reports that were lacking in simple but important information. When appraising a complete business it is important to specify who retained the appraiser, the full legal name of the corporation, and what state it was incorporated in. Many appraisal reports do not clearly specify what interest in the entity is being appraised and sometimes the effective date of the appraisal is unclear.

The standard of value (i.e., fair market value, fair value, investment value, etc.) must be clearly stated and defined. Among other factors, the business appraiser must consider the elements listed in the Internal Revenue Service Ruling 59–60. The elements generally outline the valuation of closely held stocks and include the following:

1. The nature of the business and the history of the enterprise.
2. The economic outlook in general and the condition and outlook of the specific industry in particular.
3. The book value of the stock and the financial condition of the business.
4. The company's earning capacity.
5. The company's dividend-paying capacity.
6. Whether or not the enterprise has goodwill or other intangible value.
7. Sales of stock and the size of the block to be valued.
8. The market prices of stocks of corporations engaged in the same or similar lines of business whose stocks are

actively traded in a free and open market, either on an exchange or over-the-counter.

In a business appraisal, correct adjustments to the financial statements are imperative. Appraisers can fail to recognize adequate reserves for such allowances as doubtful accounts receivables. Adjustments to inventory for obsolete or damaged stock is also important.

One of the most common mistakes in adjusting the financial statements of a company is failure to remove nonrecurring items in order to *normalize* earnings. Some examples would be gains or losses from the sale of assets, losses from a major catastrophe, insurance recovery proceeds, and gains or losses from a settlement of a lawsuit. Many appraisers will go into great detail comparing the subject business with industry averages, but leave the reader to his own conclusion as to the results. In other words they do not fully explain the company's strengths or weaknesses as compared to the ratios of similar companies. The results of the financial statement analysis should come to some kind of conclusion concerning the degree of risk that is associated with the subject company as compared to other similar companies in its industry.

Most importantly the appraisal must be such that it is clear, step-by-step, as to how the appraiser reached his conclusion. It should be such that the reader can duplicate the appraiser's steps and reach the same conclusion. In my opinion, this is the most common error that appraisers in any discipline make. Most appraisers narrate and reach conclusions as if they were writing a report for another appraiser. They assume that the reader has the same knowledge of valuation as they do. Each valuation method should have a step-by-step explanation of all calculations and a discussion of the purpose that the method should address.

In many reports, if read closely, some appraisers will contradict their own conclusion or at least appear to. A common example of this is in the discussion of the industry in general and the final outlook for the subject company. I have seen reports where the appraiser's research into the industry in general left the reader with a bleak outlook for the future and later in the report discuss how the company should continue to prosper. This may indeed be the case, but the appraiser must discusses why the subject business will prosper when the industry in general is down.

Another common mistake in business valuation is lack of emphasis on critically important issues. Appraisers will include countless pages in their report developing the earnings base of the company and address only briefly how they arrived at the capitalization rate. Just as important, the appraiser will use countless appraisal methods and then conclude with a final value without explaining which method or combination of methods were used and why that method or combination of methods were used.

Another common error is the use of rules of thumb methods, and in some cases they are used as the final valuation method in arriving at a value. I have seen several reports that included only rules of thumb methods. These were used mainly by appraisers that specialized in only one industry. While these rules of thumb may be helpful in certain industries, I can never believe that they should be relied on as a final conclusion of value.

One of the most common errors in appraisal, mainly in real estate appraisal, is adjustments for comparable sales. Many reports leave the reader with little knowledge of how the appraiser developed the adjustment. Each adjustment that is made in comparing sales for time, location, and size must be calculated and explained in such a way that the reader can reach the same conclusion.

The appraiser must also research the circumstances surrounding the comparable sales. Sales that are distressed or sales whereby a property owner paid in excess of market value for property desperately needed, such as a lot for additional parking next to his business, or sales between relatives must all be adjusted and explained to the reader. Many real estate appraisers will list all of the types of sales previously discussed and then take an average. This is generally a mistake. Sales that require too many adjustments should not be heavily relied on but can serve as the limits to a range of values. Those sales that are the closest in all respects to the subject are the most meaningful.

Many machinery and equipment appraisers fail to adequately discuss the market for the type of equipment they are appraising. Other common errors in machinery and equipment appraisal are failing to list the sources of research from which the values were derived. Most important is to list the condition of the equipment and in some cases how long it has been working. Imperative is a good description of each condition rating and the depth of the on-site inspection. The report must also include a good discussion of how the appraiser reached his conclusion concerning the condition of the equipment, since most appraisers are only visually inspecting the equipment.

Another common mistake in machinery and equipment appraisals is failure to adequately describe each piece of equipment and where the equipment is located. I have seen appraisals on oil rigs whereby the appraiser obviously did not understand the market. An example of this is the pricing of a rig by its component parts. The value of the component or supporting equipment will not always be the value of the total rig as a package. The reason for this is that most component parts of a rig are sold at auction or this is the market with which the equipment competes. Therefore it is very unlikely that the sum of the parts when valued in this method would equal the value of a total rig, assembled together and working.

In most cases rigs are sold as a package and this is the value that the client is requesting. Location of the rig sometimes has an important impact on the value and many machinery and equipment appraisers will make an adjustment for this factor. The main influence on the valuation of the rig is by means of comparable sales. However, when the rig is priced in this manner very few appraisers will even address where the appraiser obtained the data.

In summary, the overall problem that most appraisers are guilty of is the failure to present the steps in the appraisal process and the methodology in terms that a layman can understand. In other words, we fail to understand that the reader of the report is not another appraiser.

EXPERT WITNESS TESTIMONY

1. Qualifications to become an expert witness.

    There are no qualifications to become an expert witness other than a judge, after reading your credentials, qualifies you as an expert. Once this has been done, you are an expert witness. In other words, all it takes is for one judge to qualify you as an expert.

2. Preparation.

    (a) Know your report. I cannot emphasize enough the importance of going over your report thoroughly prior to taking the witness stand. In most cases the report has been done several months ago and sometimes years prior to the court hearing. Therefore you must revisit every aspect of the report so that you are as familiar with it as the day you finished writing it. Believe me, the opposing attorney and his advisors will be.

(b) Know the reason for every conclusion and be able to support it. The following ruling by the IRS may seem to put most appraisers at ease about information they relied upon in reaching their conclusion. However, there are some key phrases that a sharp attorney can use to discredit a good appraiser if the appraiser has been negligent in keeping good documentation to support his or her opinion. Rule 703 of the Federal Rules of Evidence states:

> The facts or data in the particular case upon which an expert bases an opinion or inference may be those perceived by or made known to him at or before the hearing. If of a type reasonably relied upon by experts in the particular field in forming opinions or inferences upon the subject, the facts or data need not be admissible in evidence.

Analyzed, it is the opinion of the expert that is the evidence, not the hearsay information that supports it.

(c) Write down the questions for your attorney to ask you and instruct him to ask only those.

Most attorneys are not that familiar with business appraisal and, if the questions are left up to your attorney, he may unknowingly ask you questions that give the opposing attorney ammunition to attack a part of your testimony. Always instruct or give your attorney the questions to ask you while on the witness stand.

(d) Try to anticipate the questions that the opposing attorney will ask you and make sure you will have the correct answers.

Because appraisal is not an exact science, the appraiser is forced to make some subjective conclusions. Focus in on these and try to find as much research or logic as possible to support the conclusions that are subjective.

(e) Mentally and physically play out the court scene. Watch your posture and gestures. If you have never watched yourself in a video under pressure you will be amazed at your body language and the quirks that you never realized you had. Visualize the type of posture, personality, and charisma that you want to portray and force yourself to become that character.

3. The deposition.

(a) The opposing attorney will subpoena your file prior to the deposition.

Be extremely careful about what you keep in your files. Again, most attorneys are not well versed in business appraisal and therefore the only way to combat your testimony is to discredit you or something in your report. The slightest note written on a document can cause an avalanche attack on your credibility whether it has anything to do with the final value or not.

(b) The deposition rules are similar to court proceedings.

Depositions are usually conducted in a courtlike fashion with a court reporter to take down every word of the deposition. It is not uncommon for the deposition to be videotaped. Because it is not held in a court of law and the setting begins rather informally (this is to set you up usually), an appraiser will say more than he needs to or does not thoroughly think through his answers. The answers in the deposition must be in keeping with what you plan to say in court. Actually at this point, the less information you give out the better. If possible, only answer yes and no and do not volunteer any information unless absolutely necessary. It is important to also set up the opposing attorney from the appraiser's side by not trying to overwhelm him with how brilliant you are. It is better to let him think that you are not that convincing in court. This may tend to make the opposing attorney not overprepare for the attack that is coming in the courtroom.

Also, demand that your attorney provide you with the transcript of the deposition and study it very thoroughly prior to the court hearing. You can bet the opposing attorney will almost memorize it word-for-word and will make an unbelievable case with just a small discrepancy from what you said in the deposition. With very little effort the opposing attorney can get a transcript of every court testimony you have given in the past, and will confront you with any discrepancies from prior testimonies. Be able to defend any changes from any testimony from the past to assumptions you are making currently. Close attention to what the opposing attorney is focusing on may give you a clue about what he has read in a prior case that he is setting you up for when you finally take the stand.

(c) Attend the opposing expert's deposition to determine any weaknesses and to help plan your presentation.

Your attorney will definitely be at that hearing and you have every right to be there as a consultant to your attorney. This is where you want to help your attorney pick out the flaws or weaknesses in the other appraiser's opinion. Do not talk, as you are only a consultant to your attorney, but keep good notes that you can discuss afterward with your attorney to put him on the right track to attack the other appraiser's testimony in court. In court, it is very simple: whoever is discredited loses.

(d) Paying careful attention to the opposing attorney will help you detect the types of questions he will ask you in court.

During both depositions (yours and the opposing appraiser's) pay close attention to every word that the opposing attorney is asking. Many times you can pick out the path or the target from the opposing attorney, what he feels are important assumptions in the opinion of value. This is usually what he will be attacking in court. If you have a good sense of what the attorney is focusing on, you can also focus your testimony and research to back up your answers.

(e) Be courteous, but as brief as possible in your answers so that you can elaborate in court if necessary without contradicting yourself.

Never be cocky or deviate from total professionalism. Your portrayal should be one of confidence and courtesy, no matter how hard the attack.

(f) Carefully frame all of your answers.

This is not a court deposition, and pauses don't show up in the transcript, so take your time before answering. Most importantly, never answer a question you do not fully understand. You can ask the attorney to rephrase the question as many times as you want so that you fully understand what he or she is asking.

You have plenty of time to check your answers from information in your files.

4. Court testimony.

    (a) Dress conservatively.

It is extremely important to dress conservatively and professionally. It is so critical that the larger law firms will require you to dress accordingly and will usually send in someone to check your appearance. Although it may not seem so important to you, it is important to the court and how they perceive your testimony.

    (b) You are allowed to bring your files and any notes or presentation material with you on the witness stand.

The very last question that you should instruct your attorney to ask you is "How did you arrive at your opinion?" This is where you want to conduct a class on the valuation that you did. Most importantly, speak in layman's terms. Never try to talk above the court in appraisal language and make sure that every assumption you state is backed up with everyday, easy-to-understand examples. By explaining the methodology in very general terms and relating it to the normal buyer's everyday finances helps the court understand the assumption. For instance, if you were explaining a capitalization rate, relate it to a money market fund or bank rates, then explain why you added your risk factors.

Another way to relate to capitalization rates is by way of a multiple of earnings. In essence, when you speak of a multiple of earnings, what you are really saying is that a buyer wants his money back in a certain amount of years. If the business has a history of ups and downs, then it is hard for a buyer to feel comfortable about the future, so therefore you might relate a 33% cap rate to a multiple of three years' earnings. In other words, a buyer, based on the historical ups and downs of the company, cannot foresee anymore than three years down the road and thus would want his money back in three years. This type of explanation is not only understandable and logical to the court but makes it very hard for the opposing attorney to attack your logic.

Keep in mind that any presentation materials need to be presented to the opposing side prior to using them in court, unless you are using a chalkboard.

(c) Your testimony should usually follow the logical steps in your appraisal.

  (i)   Usually the first thing your attorney will want you to do is explain your qualifications.

Carefully prepare the presentation about yourself to elaborate on areas of your qualifications that are pertinent to the valuation assignment and will make you appear as an expert in the areas that support your assumptions.

  (ii) Description of the assignment.

For example: I was employed by Mr. Smith to give an opinion of fair market value on ABC company.

Explain what is valued. If the company is a corporation explain what is to be valued and what assets would be involved.

  (iii) Conclusion of value. State the value at which you have arrived.

(iv) Explain the steps carried out in arriving at the value.

For example: On October 18, 1997, I visited the ABC company and inspected all of the assets noting their condition. I interviewed Mr. James Brown, the company's comptroller. I learned from this interview that ___.

I researched the economic climate of the overall industry and the company's trade area to aid me in the forecasting for the company. I found ___.

I analyzed and made adjustments to the balance sheet in order to bring the following assets to a fair market value instead of their book value which reflects values for tax purposes only.

I made adjustments to the profit and loss statements to better reflect the true earning power of the company. In order to do this I adjusted ___.

(v) Briefly but fully, and without getting complicated, explain the various methods that you used in arriving at your value, and most importantly why you chose the methods you felt were most appropriate for this type of company.

(vi) Explain your value conclusion in such a way that a lay person will understand. Bring it to a level of common sense.

For example: I feel this value is reasonable because it represents the value of the company's assets and approximately one year's net profit to the owner.

5. Cross examination.

The opposing attorney's job is to discredit you as an expert. He usually does not understand business valuation.

The types of questions he will ask will be those that are complicated and leave a certain impression, usually wrong, that you can only answer with a yes or no.

(a) No sarcastic or smart answers.

Always remain professional and in control no matter how difficult the attack from the other side may be. Never answer with a sarcastic or rude answer. Remain unshakable! The more you remain unshakable, the harder the other attorney will try to attack and the more ridiculous he or she will look to the court. In most cases a constant attack on you frustrates the opposing attorney when he can't get to you. It often makes the court feel that the attorney is groping for anything, and doesn't really have any strategy except to pick on you, and not the value at which you arrived.

(b) Direct your answers and presentation to the judge. You are there to educate the court.

Most attorneys cannot stand it when you address the judge with your answers to their questions. However, it is the court you are there to inform; if this frustrates the opposing attorney and he complains, simply state that you were under the impression that you were there to inform the court. This will usually frustrate him even more, because he cannot correct you on this. However, keep in mind that you do not want to do these things in a sarcastic tone or to appear being rude.

Act as if you simply thought this was the way things were done in court and were showing respect for the judge. I realize that most of what I have previously said is directed toward frustrating the opposing attorney, but if you can rattle him or her, it makes it hard for them to focus on discrediting you. A calm attorney will have a line of questions that will eventually make you look like an idiot at the end of his attack. Unless you rattle or frustrate him, he can usually weaken your testimony.

(c) Your rights.

You may ask the opposing attorney to rephrase his questions as many times as you like if you do not understand what he is asking. You have the right to clarify the answer and you should ask to be allowed to do so if failure to clarify would leave a misrepresentation. If this is not allowed then you can answer the question by saying, "If I understand your question, you are asking me ___," then answer the way you want.

For example: My answer is yes, if you are asking me ___.

The opposing attorney will only ask you questions that he knows the answer to, never bet otherwise.

(d) Watch for setup circles.

These are a line of questions that usually seem reasonable, but are leading you in a circle to contradict yourself at the end. You will be amazed at how good most attorneys are at this.

(e) Your attorney will usually not object to anything and, usually, will sit there and let you get beat up.

This has always amazed me, but it usually happens. Remember, most attorneys do not understand business appraisal and therefore may not know what to object to. In time, you can brief your attorney on areas that he should object to that have nothing to do with the valuation. For example, the attack on your credentials. I have had my attorney stand up and object to this saying that "this line of questioning is irrelevant and a waste of the court's time, as the witness has already been qualified and been accepted by the court as an expert."

VALUING INTANGIBLE ASSETS

There are many reasons to include the valuation of intangible assets connected with a business. The major ones are allocation of the purchase price and the transfer of ownership. Most buyers will want the intangible assets identified and valued for amortization purposes. When transferring ownership, rights to individual assets may be either transferred or gifted, but must have a value.

Intangible assets may consist of proprietary lists containing customers, clients, or patients. These are valuable where the relationship is ongoing. Beneficial contracts also have an intangible value if the company is selling a product or service at a higher markup than a noncontract customer, or it is purchasing or leasing at a rate below what it might pay without the contract. Generally it can be amortized over the length of the contract. Patents and patent applications are another example of an intangible asset. Patents have two life spans—legal and economic. The shorter of the two should be used. Patent attorneys may feel that the legal life span ends before the seventeenth year because of the time involved in enforcing the patent rights. The most common method of valuing the patent is the discounted cash flow method, but consult an expert.

Copyrights have long legal life spans but short economic

life spans. For example, books have a copyright of the author's life plus 50 years. Trademarks and brand names also have value if they allow the company to sell its product at a higher price than the similar product of its competitors. Trademarks do not have a determinable life and therefore cannot be amortized. Franchise and territorial agreements are another example of intangible assets. Franchise agreements have more value the longer they have been in existence and the better its name recognition, however, they usually cannot be amortized because their lives cannot be determined. Territorial agreements are a form of monopoly and their value increases with the length of time and their exclusivity. Likewise, they cannot be amortized unless they have a specific time frame and the supplier has a policy of not renewing the agreement.

Software has value when it is unique to that company and allows it to operate more efficiently than its competitor. If its life span can be determined, then it can be amortized.

Goodwill is generally regarded as those factors which generate repeat business such as reputation or location.

One of the methods used to value intangibles is the cost to create. This is the cost to duplicate a given asset at the present time, but does not measure future contribution to profit. An example of this would be software developed for/by a company to manage its inventory, but not in the business of selling software. Another method used is the capitalization of income. This is used to value expected earnings over a period of time.

The capitalization rate should reflect the risks involved. A customer list would be best valued this way. The discounted cash flow method is used exclusively when the predictable life span and the future economic benefit of the asset can be determined. Examples of this would be subscriptions, service contracts, or patents with royalty payments.

EXAMPLES OF INTANGIBLE ASSETS

Film and record libraries

Loan portfolio

Easement rights

Patents and patent application

License agreements

Royalty agreements

Purchase contracts

Leases

Franchise agreements

Noncompetitive agreement

Employment contracts

Engineering drawing and specifications

Service contracts

Brand names

Backlog of orders

Insurance agency expirations

Contracts with customers

Performance rights

Advertisers

Core depositor relationships

Favorable financing

Distributorship

Product lines

Proprietary technology

Consumer software

Supply contrasts

Formulas

Trade names

Copyrights

Mailing lists

Subscribers

Publishing rights

Film rights

Water rights

Medical records

Goodwill

Mortgage service rights

Insurance agency force

VALUING ASSETS

Most individuals involved in selling and/or appraisal of complete companies usually underestimate the importance of the fair market value of the assets of the business. Many appraisers and intermediaries merely rely on *book value* or the owner's best estimate, or even an arbitrary discount or premium based on the type of asset involved. The theory of not really doing a value analysis on the assets is mainly derived by the assumption that the business is worth what the market will pay, or in other words its *fair market value*, and that the assets are merely the basis for producing the income stream. It is also a common philosophy that because goodwill is the difference between the assets and the company's fair market value, that if you are slightly off on the value of the assets, the only factor influenced is that the company will show more or less intangible value, but the fair market value of the complete business is still the same.

If you look into the accepted methods that are used to value businesses, several aspects begin to cloud the above scenario. For instance, appraisers do, and should, use historical as well as projected financial analysis to normalize discretionary net profit. Correctly done, a deduction from projected profits for the cost of new equipment (capital additions) to handle future increases in revenues for the business in the projected years and a deduction for true (sometimes called economic depreciation or a capital reserve) depreciation for historical years are necessary to arrive at a true earnings picture of the company now and in the future. In normalizing the income stream for historical and projected years, keep in mind that at a capitalization rate of 25%, every $1,000 of discretionary net profit can equal four times that amount when capitalizing the income, thereby having a drastic impact on the overall value of the company.

Another aspect that one must consider is that many of the calculations in the various methods take into consideration the value of the assets. Those that are not directly impacted by methodology involving the assets are still derived from capitalization of the income stream, and as stated above can result in some drastic differences in value. One of the most popular methods used by intermediaries and appraisers is a combination of assets plus a multiple of earnings, or mainly just a multiple of earnings associated with the type of business being valued. Almost all accepted methodology relies on the normalized income stream. Again, assets can play a significant role in the overall estimate of value of the business. Depending on the size of the company and the various methods used, an error in valuing the assets can have more of an effect than one might think. Also, although most business appraisers *do not* value the real estate, one must be certain to research this asset to determine the fair market rent to be deducted from expenses.

When discussing hard assets, there are various categories such as furniture, fixtures and equipment, vehicles or rolling stock, inventory (both for resale and parts for everyday repairs), leasehold improvements, as well as licenses, patents, and trademarks. Each category of assets has to be analyzed individually and some research is required. Keep in mind that in addition to the fair market value of each item, you may have to arrive at a *value in use* of the equipment. Value in use is defined as the value of an economic good to its owner/user is based on the production (privacies in income; utility or amenity form) of the economic good to a specific individual. This is a subjective value however, and may not necessarily represent market value.

When valuing furniture, fixtures, and equipment, several things can happen. For instance, you will usually encounter two scenarios that stand out when consulting used equipment dealers, sometimes auctioneers (although you are mainly looking for fair market value, in some cases auction value is the market), and trade association magazine classified ads as well as the owner's own estimate and owners of similar businesses; one is that everyone seems to know the value of the various pieces of equipment or that no one can give you a straight answer until they see the equipment and its condition. In most cases, it is wise to add an expense budget to your valuation fee to research these items or to have a competent equipment dealer come out and value each piece separately. This is usually a nominal fee for a value per item, estimated at a retail selling price.

It is also wise to consult the owner and find out his value per item, as well as to ask him who he would buy used equipment from. You may use this source to get a second opinion. Also, ask the owner for the last month's issue of his trade association magazine and locate a list of other dealers in the classified section. This will also give you the phone number of the trade association. Obtain a reference from the trade association on one of its members who is considered an expert on equipment values or one who is the largest in the industry. Call this individual and explain that you were referred by his trade association as being an expert on equipment (flattery will get you everywhere in this case) and are checking values on the assets of a company you are performing an evaluation on that is smaller than his. In most cases, because you have flattered him, he will give you more information than you probably bargained for. If he is not that familiar with the equipment, he will give you carte blanche to the department head that purchases equipment for his company. He may even show an interest in the purchase of the company, but be firm and ethical. Due to confidential agreements that you signed with the company, say that you can give no information until it is valued, packaged, and the owner has agreed to place it on the market. However, you can assure him that he will be the first person you contact, because of his help. He will definitely respect you for your efforts and in many cases it is not uncommon for him to call you back to value his company to sell or give you a referral from someone in the same business that offered their company to him.

Always keep a separate form for recording what each contact has estimated for each piece of equipment so that you have a range to use based on the condition of the equipment. This also gives you a supportable document that you can refer back to should someone question your values. Once you have completed this, you can adjust the equipment on the balance sheet by adding to or deducting from depreciation to reflect the fair market value of the assets. This gives you an economic adjustment that is based on fair market value rather than a taxed based value as set forth by IRS schedules. Taxed based values are usually only for tax purposes and usually do not reflect the true value of the equipment.

In the second scenario, where hardly anyone knows the value of the equipment until they see it, this is an indication that age, condition, and model has a significant impact on value. Although each (including the owner) dealer or contact may not be sure what the equipment is worth, all will definitely know how long each piece of equipment will last. This is where the *remaining useful life* (RUL) method applies best. Again, keep notes about who you talk to and their estimate of useful life of each piece of equipment.

Based on a range of life expectancy, you can deduct a fair and reasonable life for each piece of equipment. The calculations are a simple mathematical method of redoing the depreciation schedule that the accountant has prepared. Sometimes you will find that the depreciation schedules the accountant has prepared accurately represent the true life expectancy of the equipment and therefore do not need adjustment. This is usually true in hi-tech electrical or computerized equipment. In most cases this is not the case and a new depreciation schedule must be established from the research you have collected. An example of the methodology and calculations to determine the value (again, sometimes referred to as changing it to an economic depreciation value) would be, for instance, in a restaurant. The accountant has used a seven-year life on a stove, when the true life expectancy of that stove is at least 15 years and the original cost was $2,000. Therefore, if the owner paid $2,000 and has used it for 5 years, then this piece of equipment has a remaining useful life of 10 more years. The calculations are as follows: $2,000 divided by 15 years equals 133.33 per year in loss of value. With 10 years left it is a simple calculation; the stove is worth $1,333. ($133.33 × 10 years = $1,333.) Since the accountant's value on the books is $750 ($2,000 divided by 8 years × 3 more years of life) or ($2,000 – $750 = $1,250 in depreciation), you can add back $583 to the $1,250. This will add a positive $667 to reflect a depreciation of $583 to the minus $1,250. Therefore $2,000 (original cost) minus $667 = $1,333.

This simple mathematics must be judged by the condition of the equipment. The preceding example assumes that the equipment is in good condition and has been routinely maintained. However, some equipment may have been severely abused or neglected and have no ongoing maintenance program in place, thus forcing the appraiser to lower the remaining useful life. Although this seems extremely subjective, the following criteria, based on common sense, should be helpful in determining condition.

Definitions of Conditions

The following definitions of conditions have been developed for use by business evaluation systems. They are intended to promote a good understanding of conditions assigned to items appraised and an effective means of communicating the impact of condition on value. Care must be taken in assignments of condition ratings to accurately reflect the impact on value.

Excellent
New, near new, or practically new mechanical condition, extremely low hours of use, no defects, and may still be under warranty.

Very Good
Exceptionally good condition. May have just recently been completely overhauled or rebuilt with new or near new materials and/or has had such limited use that no repairs or worn part replacements are necessary. Very low hours of use.

Good
In complete 100% operating condition. No known or obvious mechanical defects but may have some minor worn parts that will need repair or replacement in the near future. May have high hours of use but no defects are obvious.

Fair
Has very high hours or extended use. Defects are obvious and will require repair or general rebuild soon. Not 100% functional or efficient, may be operational or functional but questionable.

Poor
Has seen very hard and long hours of service. Requires rebuilding, repair, or overhaul before it can be used. Not operational or functional.

Scrap

Cost of repair exceeds value or cost of replacing with like/
kind equipment. Beyond useful or functional life and should
be sold as scrap.

Condition Codes (E) (V) (G) (F) (P) (S)

Determining Conditions

It should be noted that in determining conditions, the appearance of the particular item is important. However, the equipment must be judged on mechanical and electrical working
conditions and not just on appearance. Paint, lubrication, and
general cleanup should be part of general maintenance and
should not be used to cover up defective equipment. The
appraiser must use experience and firsthand knowledge of
the equipment to make accurate judgments for condition
ratings.

The physical condition, deterioration, depreciation, or
state of repair is a major factor in values. Loss of value due
to curable or incurable depreciation is a consideration of
market value.

Please keep in mind the element of common sense, and
if possible obtain a repair schedule or a maintenance schedule. For instance, sometimes in the case of oilfield equipment, although an engine or drawworks on a rig may appear
to be in severe need of repair, check with the head of maintenance and you may find that after every so many hours,
that piece of equipment is pulled and completely rebuilt and
the parts are in the warehouse ready for this repair. Now, what
you have is an engine that is in *poor* condition, but all of the
new parts are in the warehouse and it is scheduled to be totally
rebuilt soon, and this is a normal expense represented in the

profit and loss statements and treated as a normal cost of doing business. How would you rate this? The answer is *good,* since it is running and the parts to rebuild it are already in the warehouse and labor is an everyday function of the repair department. Be extremely careful when valuing leasehold improvements. Buyers will not pay for used leasehold improvements if they can get a new *build out* for free in a similar space. Also, if the owner didn't pay for improvements— neither should the buyer.

Assuming the current owner paid for leasehold improvements and the local lease market is not providing spaces built to the tenant's specifications, use the following schedules:

Long-Lived Improvements (10- to 25-year life)
Walls, electrical wiring, and plumbing can be valued at the original cost of installation with no deduction for depreciation. (Inflation rates will compensate for depreciation.)

Intermediate-Lived Improvements (5- to 10-year life)
Signs, water heaters, air conditioners, air compressors, furnaces, and so on. Use a *straight line depreciation* based on actual useful life.

Disposable or Fashionable (0- to 5-year life)
Carpeting, blinds, draperies, and other decorative items are subject to rapid wear and fashion trends. They will be worth 75% of original cost if in new condition, 50% of original cost if in good condition, 25% of original cost if in fair condition, and 0% of original cost if in worn condition.

In the case of vehicles or rolling stock, there are three good sources for price information:

1. *Blue Book Value.* This guide is available at many bookstores for a nominal fee and is extremely reliable.

2. *Classified ad.* Many local publications and newspapers advertise vehicles and the average price from a number of ads will represent the prevailing market.

3. *Depreciation schedule model.* Minimum value is 20% of original cost. Enter mechanical equipment original value, then deduct accumulated depreciation. The total is the mechanical equipment value. Remember 20% of cost in most cases is the minimum.

Every business normally has some inventory of stock for internal use or products for resale. The actual value of stocks or inventory is usually determined by a physical inventory completed the day the business sale is consummated. You can use the following sources for information:

1. Have a professional inventory service determine market value.

2. Use last year's tax statement to find your *ending inventory* and *beginning inventory.*

Be careful, since many people make year-end adjustments to inventory levels for tax purposes. Look for the value on a *normal day.*

Environmental Due Diligence

There is a relatively new discipline in the field of environmental studies known as environmental due diligence. It involves aspects that, as of yet, have not been fully defined. This uncertainty can cause an extra set of problems for those of us involved in business transfers, consulting, and appraisals. One hears much about the superfund, but one of the main purposes of the fund is to impose liability on parties responsible for contamination by hazardous substance releases. The few exceptions to this liability are the second creditor exemption and the innocent landlord defense. The latter requires "all appropriate inquiry into the previous ownership and uses of the property consistent with good commercial or customary practice." The definition of *appropriate* and *good commercial* or *customary practice* is presently left to the courts. The lack of a consistent definition leads to a lack of standards in the environmental due diligence process.

Environmental due diligence studies are carried out in phases by trained certified professionals; as the phases progress, the cost rises. The screening phase, or Prephase I stage, involves the initial environmental assessment in which suspicion of contamination is addressed. If there is no evidence of prior contamination, a Phase I study is deemed unnecessary; if the assessment indicates that a Phase I study is necessary, or if the state regulations mandate further investigation, the investigator must begin a due diligence environmental audit covering a records search and an initial site inspection to determine evidence of prior contamination. If there is no evidence of contamination, it is not necessary to continue the due diligence study; however, if contamination is found, the investigator must then proceed to a Phase II or intrusive study stage. In this stage, the actual sampling and analysis of the site occurs. If tests indicate that hazardous substances are present at levels detrimental to human health, or the environment, a Phase III study must be undertaken. This final phase is also known as the cleanup, or corrective action phase and involves remediation of on-site contamination to protect human health and the environment.

Buyers, sellers, and lenders (the three main parties involved in a property transaction) have unique interests, yet all require environmental due diligence investigations to be performed. Even though the overall objective of a property transaction is to consummate the deal, each party will have a distinct agenda. Lenders maintain the most varying position of the three in that they may buy or sell property, or lend money for a transaction. Insurance companies, for example, may lend money to outside investors, or maintain their own real estate investments. Thus, they are active buyers and sellers of commercial and industrial properties, as well as lenders to other property buyers.

Buyers of commercial and industrial properties may be required by law to conduct a prephase due diligence study. At this time New Jersey, Illinois, and Connecticut are the only states to strictly require a property transfer assessment; although further states are expected to follow suit, many buyers still view the due diligence process as an unnecessary expense required by the lender. Cautious buyers will no doubt accept the cost of the environmental due diligence audit regardless of lender requirements. Prepurchase evaluation of a business property site will help minimize risks and possibly identify problems prior to title transfers, thereby reducing the financial risk. For example, indemnifications force the seller to either retain liability, divide liability between the buyer and seller, or have the seller retain the contaminated portion of the property. As a result of the due diligence examination, the buyer obtains some leverage with which to negotiate the financial terms of the transaction to cover possible environmental risks.

Lenders will also require this evaluation prior to foreclosure of a property, since foreclosure can cause them to be considered owners or operators of the facility and bear liability for any necessary site cleanup action.

Investment banks, in the financing of mergers and acquisitions, are also susceptible to environmental liabilities of their borrowers, although they do not currently incorporate environmental due diligence as a requirement of financing, and they have not been receptive to the environmental review process. However, they and the venture capitalists will no doubt be increasingly pressured to comply with due diligence as a standard.

Since a legal opinion on environmental compliance is increasingly becoming a requirement for property transfers, attorneys representing buyers are insisting upon the completion of environmental due diligence studies prior to closing a particular transaction. It is well known that environmental problems at a property site can be assumed by successor owners, and that resolving environmental problems can be expensive. Therefore, prudent attorneys advise their clients to investigate potential liabilities. Should problems be identified, the attorney can incorporate protective measures (indemnifications, covenants, hold backs, etc.) into the formal purchase agreement.

Because of the lack of standards for due diligence investigations, an intense review of the facility background information as well as the facilities history is critical.

The environmental due diligence study involves numerous areas of inquiry: The history of regulatory compliance and response to permit requirements; hazardous waste liabilities due to past or current practices associated with the use, storage, treatment, or disposal of hazardous materials or substances on or near the subject site; past or current off-site hazardous waste disposal practices, and a history of regulatory compliance and response to permit requirements.

The evaluation of potential on-site hazardous waste contamination is generally achieved using a phased investigation approach. The Phase I investigation is used to identify potential problems. This does not usually include analytical testing but does determine the need for any follow-up testing, such as soil, tank tightness, or ground water analysis. This information is obtained via documents research, inspection of the property, and interviews with facility personnel and regulatory officials.

Investigation of the site is perhaps the most important aspect of the due diligence investigations. Although a title search is important in determining *use*, it is not ownership that is the key. Determining past uses of a property helps to identify potentially hazardous materials and wastes that may have been present.

Some potential indicators of hazardous waste problems are: discolored soil; dead or stressed vegetation; spills around loading docks, fuel areas, and surface drains; stained or discolored sinks, drains, or sumps; discolored or turbid surface water on property; wetlands, streams, drainage ditches, rivers, lagoons, and retention ponds. Other indicators can be noxious odors and/or leaks from pipes, electrical transformers, tanks, barrels, or containers.

A review of governmental permits, inspection and compliance, and incident response records is another step in investigating the facility. It is most important to find out if the facility is a federal or state licensed hazardous waste generator, storage unit, transporter, or disposer and what wastes are involved and if any governmental inspections have occurred. Another aspect to explore is the likelihood of underground tanks on the property, and if so, what are their characteristics. A check at the local fire department, town hall license records, state underground tank registration, and Sandborn Fire Insurance Maps will reveal when the tanks were installed.

Off-site contingent liabilities are a major concern in that superfund sites generally involve abandoned dumps and a number of major corporations have been named as potentially responsible parties (PRPs) relating to one or more superfund sites. Some sites involve several hundred PRPs. Current PRPs' involvement with federal or state superfund sites can be determined through the following: EPA's Comprehensive Environmental Response, Compensation, and Liability Act Information System (CERCLIS) database and comparable state databases; EPA's PRP database; company files to identify current and past disposal locations; and a review of the Security and Exchange Commissions (SEC) 10-K submissions.

Even though due diligence studies are not mandatory at this time (except in New Jersey, Illinois, and Connecticut), on-site regulatory compliance includes liability for on-site hazardous waste problems. If an environmental compliance audit is not practical because of time and cost, a preliminary environmental due diligence examination should still address the following questions: Are the required permits federal, state, or local? Is the subject facility operating with the required permits? Are there any notices of violations or enforcement actions in the facility's files?

Although in most states due diligence studies are not required, this does not mean that those consultants and advisors or agents associated with a business or real property transfer are not responsible for any liability that may occur after the sale. Recently in a precedent-setting case in Wisconsin, the court ruled that an appraiser, retained by a bank, should have seen evidence of waste-oil contamination that was later spotted in a visual survey of the property. The case, *Horicon State Bank vs. Karit Lumber Co.*, was over a property the bank acquired in a bankruptcy process.

This is one more indication that appraisers and other professionals are being held responsible for making note of environmental issues. In this case there was a very obvious sign of environmental problems that the court felt a professional appraiser should have been able to make a note of in a report to the client. The court also reprimanded the lender for not having an environmental assessment performed. Keep in mind that the liability of environmental contamination does not fall only on the owner of the property but can extend to others not having ownership in the property. Some companies not having ownership in property may be equally liable as potentially responsible parties (PRPs), thus eluding the eye of an untrained professional advisor, broker, or agent assisting in the transfer of the business or property.

ANALYZING AND RECASTING
FINANCIAL STATEMENTS

There is no way, other than a thorough analysis of the income stream and expense flow, to justify and estimate the true value of a company, nor should there be. Most individuals understand the basic difference between public companies and private companies, but most forget that a public company's daily routine is to try to show as much profit as possible. To the converse, management of a private company strives to make as much profit daily, but tries to show the least it can for tax purposes. Most good accountants accomplish this well for private companies, but what shows on the bottom line for tax purposes, in most cases, is not the true earning capacity of the company, nor does the balance sheet actually give a fair market value of the company's assets.

The analysis and recasting process should adjust the financial statements for at least the past three years and show the true earning capacity of the company a new purchaser can expect. This is also known as *normalizing* the financial statements. Once this has been completed, a better understanding of the company's true earning capacity, or lack of it, should help the appraiser understand where the company is headed in the future. This is the most important aspect of an appraisal. Business intermediaries and appraisers sometimes forget that the driving force in the purchase of a company is the future expectation of the current income stream and not necessarily the past performance, unless it represents the likelihood of future occurrence. From this analysis, the analyst should understand where the company is needed over the next three years. In addition to recasting and analyzing the company's profit and loss statements, it is equally important to examine the balance sheet and make those adjustments to show the fair market value of the company's assets. Most of the value of the assets listed on the balance sheet are based on the best tax strategy for the company, meaning that as much depreciation as is allowable has been taken, thus lowering the value of the assets. These assets must be revalued to show the true fair market value of the assets, plus find those assets that have been written off but are still in use and have value.

In analyzing and recasting financial statements in order to quantify monetary benefits of a 100% ownership, one must decide whether to conclude with a pretax or posttax amount. If the subject company is such that it would likely be an acquisition candidate for a public company or an investing entity with the same type thinking, then a good case can be made for an after-tax conclusion.

The majority of the smaller businesses, however, tend to be either a proprietorship, partnership, or "S" corporation, each of which find the owners taxed as individuals. As a result, the acquirer of this type of company will have greater or lesser taxable income from the business than did the seller. Therefore a pretax basis of analysis permits the seller and the buyer to view the business on a like-kind basis.

Obviously all aspects of recasting and analyzing financial statements cannot be covered within the context of this chapter, but we can attempt to cover those that we are most likely to experience. We must also recognize that within the framework of Generally Acceptable Accounting Practices (GAAP) there is some latitude permitted in the preparation of financial statements.

Again it is important to note that because of this latitude in methods of accounting, while staying within the framework of acceptable practices, many closely held businesses will select those methods that maximize deductions, and thereby minimize taxable income. Large publicly traded companies try to impress shareholders and other levels of management with whom they must communicate through statements. Also, some larger corporations with nonactive shareholders will sometimes manage their earnings from year to year by switching between conservative and aggressive accounting elections in order to stabilize earnings from year to year. On the converse, however, the owner of the closely held company has no other shareholders or management to impress; therefore the statements are usually prepared with the primary goal of minimizing taxes. In addition to the accountants' financial statements there is also what is known as an economic financial statement. This is the financial statement that has been adjusted as a result of your analysis.

A closely held business whose accounting methods are designed to minimize taxes faces two negatives:

1. Their statements reflect the lowest possible profit; they are not viewed by the banking community as favorable.

2. Those same kind of statements do not impress or attract buyers.

Therefore, the analyst can be of great benefit to the company whose financial statements are designed to minimize profits, by carefully and thoroughly, through a series of adjustments, recasting the statements into a fair accurate expression of the monetary values and financial benefits of ownership. In most cases the owner of the company is the most impressed since he has probably never seen his business in this light. It is extremely important to note that the analysis and adjustments, without question, must be free of any hint of advocacy and the analyst must be able to reasonably support any adjustment. If any one thing is questionable and cannot be supported, no matter how insignificant, it will cast doubts on all adjustments and thus the economic statements will have lost their benefit. Because of this, if the analyst is not absolutely certain that he can reasonably support his adjustment, then it is better to appear conservative than risk the whole analysis to an insignificant adjustment. It is also, in my opinion, imperative that your adjusted financial statements contain a statement to the effect that the analysis and adjustments are based on the representations of the seller, without having independently audited or otherwise investigated the accuracy of those representations, and nothing you have done is intended to replace the buyer's own due diligence or decision to seek legal, accounting, or valuation counsel of his own selection.

Several aspects of the type of accounting used in preparing the financial statements must be taken into consideration. One such aspect is whether the business is on a cash basis or an accrual basis of accounting. Keep in mind that the goal of the analysis is to adjust the statements to reflect estimates of market value and levels of profits. Accrual based statements recognize assets, liabilities, income, and expenses when earned or owed, because the accounting is set up whereby the business acquires the right to receive the income or the obligation to pay the expense. Cash basis accounting only recognizes an income when paid and expenses as paid. Because of this, it is nearly always preferable to recast statements to an accrual basis.

We must also take a close look at depreciation and amortization definitions. In an economic sense, in recasting financial statements, depreciation is a loss in value of a fixed asset as a result of wear and tear or obsolescence, which cannot be corrected by normal repairs. In an accountant's financial statement, it is an expense item that permits the original cost to be written off against income over the asset's cost recovery period, as dictated from time to time by the Internal Revenue Service. When recasting the financial statements, the amount of accumulated depreciation can be much greater or much less than the amount shown on the accountant's financial statement.

The amount of depreciation taken as a noncash charge in any given period is almost always based upon the number of years approved by the IRS for cost recovery. The IRS does not estimate the useful life of assets, but only sets the number of years over which the cost of an asset may be recovered against the earning of the business. The IRS admits that the useful life of most assets is greater than the number of years they approve for cost recovery. Therefore, nearly all depreciation charges, based on the IRS's number of years of useful life, is accelerated. There are some analysts that believe that if a business uses straight line depreciation and the business did not accelerate the depreciation, that this value is equal to economic depreciation and this is false.

In an economic statement, depreciated assets must be valued at their fair market value and deductions from earnings should be considered by using a *reserve for replacement* provision. This provision recognizes the reduction in value of assets over their estimated useful life by setting aside regular funds to sufficiently meet the estimated cost of additions to replace the fixed assets when they come to the end of their useful life. (Rarely is this reserve actual money set aside for recovery when needed.) In theory, the reserve for replacement is similar to a charge for depreciation, except when used, is based on the actual loss of value rather than a cost for recovery period approved by the IRS against taxable income.

Another economic adjustment that should be made is that of interest expense. Many analysts consider interest to be a cost of capital and not an operating expense, under the assumption that the business would essentially be the same if it were debt free. This decision to treat interest as a cost of capital allows the expense to be moved down the income statement. It becomes part of *other income expense* and falls below the operating profit.

Eliminating interest from the operating expenses has an advantage to a buyer in that he or she is able to view the business on a true operating base and subtract the interest expense that would be applicable to the degree of leverage that the buyer expects to use. In most analyses of a closely held business, the given assumption is that the seller will sell on a debt-free basis and will pay all liabilities.

There are many other expenses that must also be reviewed and analyzed, such as owners compensation. Usually public companies will pay market rates for management, but a closely held company will pay whatever the business can afford and therefore must be adjusted on the economic financial statements with either a decrease or increase to net profit to reflect true market rates for the owner's services to the company. Other considerations such as rent charged to the corporation must be analyzed. In many cases the real estate and improvements in a closely held company will be owned by the owner and leased back to the corporation. In this situation, the analyst must research this expense to determine if the rent charged to the corporation truly reflects market rents in the area or if it is inflated or deflated. If one or the other exists, an increase or decrease to this expense on the economic financial statements may be in order.

Other forms of owner compensation in the way of benefits to the owner must also be analyzed to determine if these would be discretionary to alternative ownership. These are usually referred to as perquisites (perks) which are special benefits received by the owner due to the ability of the company to pay them, rather than a result of market rate compensation for services provided to the business. Some of these expenses take the form of insurance, country club memberships, boats, travel, bonuses, commissions, company-paid vehicles, vehicle maintenance and repairs, gasoline, and so on. These also must be normalized on the economic financial statement if necessary. Another expense item that must be analyzed is cost of goods sold.

Various components of this grouping will often be:

1. Direct labor.
2. Materials, and in some cases this will include freight costs for materials.
3. Subcontract labor or outside product parts or components.

In some cases transportation costs for freight can be built into the cost of goods sold line item and separated as an operating expense. This would be a double charge and should be recasted out, thus increasing income accordingly.

Also keep in mind that it is necessary to determine and analyze how inventory is valued and if the inventory value is fair market value. Some companies will operate on FIFO (first in, first out). This method is based on the assumption that the *first* unit of inventory purchased, or the *oldest*, is the first unit sold. The result of this method is that the ending inventory value is higher, therefore, the cost of goods sold is lower and in turn makes the gross profit and the net profit higher. The converse of this method sometimes used is called LIFO (last in, first out). The inventory in this method is valued on the assumption that the *last* and most recent item of inventory purchased is the first unit out of inventory to be sold. The result of this method is that the ending inventory value is lower, and therefore the cost of goods sold is higher and in turn makes the gross profit and the net profit lower.

Many analysts believe that FIFO represents a more real-world picture and when they analyze a company using LIFO, they will adjust to FIFO. If a company is using LIFO, the company's accountant should be able to provide the necessary data to adjust to a FIFO basis. In any case it is imperative that, when comparing the subject company with other similar companies, the comparable companies are using the same inventory valuation method.

Switching between methods, particularly after a highly profitable year, an owner can reduce inventory value and lower the gross and net profit. The analyst can recognize this by analyzing the income statements over several years, and if this occurred then the cost of goods sold can be adjusted to a percentage that is more typical of the other years. This should be done unless there is evidence that the lower than usual cost of goods can be reasonably anticipated to continue into the future.

Another type of expense that must be analyzed and normalized is nonrecurring expenses. Sometimes this will occur under legal and professional expenses, when the company has spent an abnormal amount due to various legal or accounting costs that are either not anticipated to reoccur or nonrelated to the actual operating expense of the company. An example of this is when the subject company may have had to sue a subcontractor or defend a lawsuit from a disgruntled partner. Other nonrecurring expenses can sometimes be found under *bad debts*.

Contributions must also be analyzed to determine what contributions would be discretionary to alternative ownership.

There are numerous other expense items as well as income items that should be adjusted and normalized, but the main intent of this discussion is to appease the reader that one of the most important exercises in valuation or preparing a company for sale is to understand exactly what the subject company's true earnings are.

REALIZED VERSUS PROJECTED EARNINGS

It seems that many individuals in mergers and acquisitions, business brokerage, business appraisal, and companies or individuals in an acquisition mode are horrified at the thought of using future projections to arrive at a realistic economic income. This thinking probably stems from the judicial system. This attitude is not without merit, since in a court of law, where evidence is all that counts, the court may not believe in an appraiser's prophecy of the future. Most business appraisers usually always assume, or should, that their appraisal will be challenged by a court or someone with an adverse opinion and interest. Therefore the use of projected business performance can and probably always will be an opposing attorney's dream to discredit the appraiser. In my opinion, it is almost a contradiction of the appraiser's assignment because it dictates performing an appraisal that will please a court of law instead of accomplishing an unbiased opinion of fair market value. Most good appraisers are hindered by this type of unrealistic thinking and in most cases may render a lower value.

The facts, in my opinion, are clear. What a business did last year is water under the bridge, and to assume it will do the same thing it did in the past is the same as assuming the future. In the real world, buyers acquire businesses in the same manner an investor buys investments. Both the price that a business buyer and the investor will pay must be an estimate of the future economic benefit of ownership that are sufficiently credible to persuade a business buyer and an investor to act on them. Granted, business buyers are very different and the circumstances surrounding a business sale versus an investment opportunity are very different, but it is the motivation that must be considered to make each act that makes them alike. I would agree that there is a substantial difference in the overall picture, since in most cases, the investor can limit his liability by his investment and can research the investment better than a buyer of a business can. The investor usually has less risk since he can usually sell his stock fairly quickly. The point is that in the real word almost everything is based on what a buyer perceives as his or her future economic benefit and that perception is what makes him/her buy or walk.

Please do not misunderstand, the analysis and reliance on historical or realized income is extremely important and is a clear vision of how the business has performed in the past. But it is not the key to value. Hardly anyone would disagree that if a business is losing money and could be a candidate for bankruptcy, very few buyers would be interested, and if they were, it would be because they thought they could purchase the business at a very low price that would reduce their risk. The converse of this is also true. If a company has performed outstanding in the past, with a healthy growth rate, many buyers would step up to the plate to make an offer, all of which would be much higher than the preceding scenario, because the perceived risk is less. But in both cases, buyers are buying because of what they perceive the past history tells them about the future, and their offers to purchase are based on the same reasoning.

The past performance of a business is the key to the value of the company and must be analyzed by the appraiser and projected into the future. This look at the future gives the appraiser a view through the buyer's eyes and that is what appraisal is all about. It is the reporting of what the market is willing to pay for an investment or a business. It is that research that tells the appraiser at what point of perceived risk the buyer is willing to act.

The capitalization of income therefore has to be based on a buyer's perception of future performance and risk. Most buyers will tell you that what they do in the future is through their own hard work and will not pay the seller for this. However, in reality, it is the seller that gave them the opportunity and momentum to accomplish their perceived goals. To me it's like saying that the touchdown had nothing to do with the coach. Certainly, it was the players that ran the play, but it was the coach that made up the play. Without the prepared play there would just be players doing their own thing, most likely in a state of confusion.

Many will tell you this is fine for a company that is either going downhill or with a perfect profitable past, but what about the company that is up in profits for one year and down the next, or a company that has stayed relatively the same for the past couple of years? This is actually a more convincing reason to use projections. The very fact that you cannot predict the future will dictate the rate to capitalize the income. Remember, you are reporting the value that makes buyers act. If you as the appraiser cannot tell what the future is going to do, then obviously a buyer is not going to risk his money for any great length of time and therefore will want his money back very quickly, thus requiring a higher capitalization rate or a lower multiple of earnings he is willing to pay for the perceived risk. That equates to a lower price. Another reason for projected earnings is that of a moral obligation to the buyer. Assume that research shows that the business has lost its most valued and profitable customer, or that legislation has been written that could adversely affect the way the business will operate, or that the company's largest supplier is going up in material costs at the first of the year.

Although bankers won't admit it, they look at the company's financials in comparison to industry standards to see how the business is doing, but the real reason is to see what the company is likely to do in the future and its ability to pay back the loan. If the bank does not perceive that, after the acquisition the company will be able to service the debt, then there is no loan, no matter how hard the buyer tries to convince the banker that he is going to do better. However, if the company shows a good profit that can easily service the debt and has been growing at a healthy rate, most likely the bank will commit on the loan.

Another case for using projections is a company we recently appraised where the business suffered greatly from the last quarter of 1994 through the end of 1995 due to expansion of the highway in front of the business. To add to the problem, the landlord, thinking that his tenants were already hurting, decided to remodel the shopping center. This also hurt the business in 1995. The company's financial statements from January 1996 through June 1996 revealed that the business had already passed the total income from 1993. Is it fair to rely on past performance or to average the historical years? What about a company that in the second quarter of 1996 signed a major five-year contract that would increase profits substantially in the future? Or what about a company that has three owners in an industry that is highly intensive on the owner's reputation and his prior dealings over the years with major clients? Is it fair to the owner or potential buyer to not take the future into consideration in order to normalize earnings and establish what picture the company will portray in the future? I cannot think of one thing that a person buys where he or she does not perceive future expectations or benefits. The real key is to measure the future in a conservative manner and give weight to those years, either past, present, or both that show the degree of occurrence for the future of the business.

In summary, the focus on the future projections, although an unconscious action on the part of the buyer, is critical. I am not advocating that the projections be shown to a buyer. To do so would almost be suicide. However, the appraisal is an opinion of value ordered by the seller. Your client is the seller and is paying you for your opinion as to what the market will pay for his or her business. The report is made to the seller and is your opinion. It is not made out to the buyer and it is the seller's property. If he chooses to show it to the buyer, then it is his property and he takes any liability that might occur.

SUMMATION OF DISCRETIONARY
NET PROFIT ANALYSIS

Again, the first step in the evaluation of a business is to reflect how you actually arrived at your discretionary net profit. This should be the result of the recasted or economic profit and loss statements as previously discussed.

It is always wise to use income tax returns for the company rather than the in-house or accountant's financial statement because this is what a potential buyer will want to see. It is the final result of the financial statements. The first step in the business evaluation research is to determine the net profit before taxes as listed on the tax returns. The rest of the *add backs* are probably obvious to you by now. However, there are some items that can be somewhat deceiving. I will try to touch on some of them again. One is owner's wages. This amount should also include the owner's payroll tax for himself. Be careful with entertainment costs. Many companies have legitimate entertainment costs that are part of their advertisement and marketing. Also, be careful with bad debts. Many companies have legitimate bad debts and they are a cost of doing business. If one year is extremely high due to something extraordinary, you may want to use an average of all the years. This is similar to *normalizing*. However, you must be careful and not appear to be *scraping the bottom of the barrel* for profit. If you feel that there is an argument for the expense to be included, then leave it alone and the final report will have more impact than if the reader feels like you are straining to find cash flow. As we stated before, usually one of the items most questioned is adding back depreciation. This is a legitimate argument, since the assets are losing value each year and at some time in the future must be replaced.

Although we are adding back the accountant's depreciation, you must subtract an amount for a true *capital reserve* that will be deducted from the cash flow.

Also remember, the most important expense that may not show up on the profit and loss statements is usually rent. If the owner owns the real estate, building, and improvements, then it is imperative that you deduct a *fair market rent* from the discretionary cash. If the owner rents the real estate and improvements to the company, then in most cases, it is higher than market rent and must be adjusted to reflect going rates for facilities similar to the subject business.

RULES OF THUMB PRICING METHODS CAN BE DANGEROUS

Rules of thumb formulas for valuing small businesses usually follow methodology involving multiples of earnings, multiples of gross sales, or a combination of sales, net profit, and/or assets.

These methods are usually very unsophisticated and involve little or no definitions of the variables or assumptions used. Although most of us use them as a quick method to determine if a seller's price is at least realistic, extreme caution must be used when we use them to help a seller price his business.

Those methods using a percentage or a multiple of gross sales have considerable inherent dangers if not balanced by good logical thinking. Take for instance the formula for a small cafe; 30% to 50% of annual gross sales. Does this mean that a small coffee shop grossing $120,000 per year, assets of $20,000, and losing $25,000 per year will sell for $36,000 to $60,000? Probably not, especially if across the street a large chain operated coffee shop has just opened. Or what if the restaurant is at the end of a long-term lease and the new rent is going to double?

Exactly what is net profit? Is it the net profit after paying income tax, or net profit before owner's salary? Most business brokers use a net profit which equates to the cash flow of the business. In other words, all expenses are deducted from income which are mandatory for the business or anyone who buys it. Other expenses that are either optional or discretionary in nature are added back to net profit since these items are controllable for a new owner. Again, such expenses are interest, depreciation, owner's salary, and can consist of others depending on the type of business involved. The problem with these formulas based on net profit is there is no definition of what net profit you are talking about. Accountants refer to net profit in mainly two different ways; net after taxes or net before taxes and interest.

Assets used in these formulas are also not defined. One does not know if the assets in these methods include real estate, cash on hand, or investments. There is a large discrepancy in value when the corporate stock is valued in comparison to an asset valuation.

When including the value of machinery, equipment, fixtures, and other *hard assets*, do you use book value, which is cost less depreciation, or do you use actual market value? It has been my experience that book value is rarely, if ever, accurate. The age of an asset and a calculation of value of loss due to age is for financial reporting. There are literally hundreds of rules of thumb to determine the value of hard assets, but there is only one sure way of determining market value. Valuing assets is a difficult subject and deserves more attention than can be covered in this chapter.

Service businesses are usually valued by a number of times the monthly gross sales, but be extremely careful in this situation. Many companies, like employee leasing firms and travel agencies, have high gross sales but only retain 5% to 10% as a gross profit. The sales price derived using these rules of thumb could literally choke the new owner with debt service.

The best use of these formulas are when they are used as a sanity check for a value derived from several of the traditional methods. These rules of thumb methods can show you a range of values that market sales have fallen between. Unless you have comparables that you are comfortable with, this is one of the least reliable ways to arrive at market value when valuing a small company.

Because these methods have become so popular with sellers and buyers, you will most likely be confronted with them. The following is a list of these rules of thumb methods, published several years ago by the American Society of Appraiser's Business Valuation Review newsletter.

Business Values Derived from Industry-related Pricing Models Based on Gross Sales

1. Accounting services—90% to 150% annual billing.
2. Answering services—13 to 16 times current monthly billing.
3. Insurance agencies—Based on the rewrite and percent of life insurance written. Valued at 125% to 200% of gross commissions.

4. Pest control—One year gross sales.

5. Travel agencies—10% of gross sales, or 1 times gross commissions.

6. Linen supplies—25 times weekly gross sales.

7. Uniform rental—35 times weekly gross sales.

8. Service businesses—X times the monthly gross income.

9. Washateria—$1,000 in value for each $100 per month gross sales.

10. Convenience stores—Often sell for a price equal to one or two months typical monthly sales, including all equipment and inventories and excluding real estate.

11. Mobile home parks—3 to 8 times typical monthly receipts which include all equipment and real estate.

12. Motels—3.69 to 4.0 times gross income based on 1978 motels sold nationally. Motels & hotels—valued at 3 to 5 times their annual gross.

13. Advertising agencies—75% of its annual gross.

14. Car washes—Full Service—valued at one times gross sales. Coin-operated car washes valued at fair market value of assets only.

15. Drive-in restaurants & cafes—Valued at 30% to 50% of annual gross sales.

16. Employment agencies—Valued at 50% of annual gross income.

Business Values Derived from Industry-related Pricing Models Based on Net Profit

1. Manufacturing or heavy-asset-related businesses—Should provide 15% to 30% return on investment, or a PE ratio (price to earnings) of 5 to 10.

Manufacturing firms—3 to 5 times net profit with the following conditions:

(a) The net profit reported to the Internal Revenue Service must be accurate and must be in addition to the salary of the owner.

(b) The company must manufacture a product, not do custom work or large government contracts.

(c) Assets must be in good condition.

(d) Must not be so technical in nature as to appeal to a very limited group of buyers.

(e) If profits are poor, then the business will sell for net worth or less.

2. Small manufacturing businesses—5 times net after tax earnings.

3. Owner-operated businesses—"X" times the owner's annual income from the business.

4. Restaurants, bars, and service-related businesses—One year's cash net profit.

5. Washateria—A price equal to 40% to 50% return on total investment if absentee owner. Example: If the price on a washateria is $23,000 and the net profit is $10,000 without the owner being the attendant, the cash return on investment is 43%, and fits the above model.

6. Accounting services—

(a) Bookkeeping services—Usually sell for .75 to 1 times the annual gross fees.

(b) Accounting practice (CPA)—Will sell for 1 to 1.25 times the annual fees.

7. Beauty shop—If staffed, will sell for one year's net profit.

8. Bakers—Wholesale—5 to 7 times the net profit.

Business Values Derived from Industry-related Pricing Models Using a Combination of Gross Sales, Net Profit, and/or Asset Value

1. Accounting services—One times annual billings plus assets.

2. General and small businesses—One year's net profit plus the principal's salary, plus inventory at cost, and the equipment at a depreciated value.

3. Bar and package liquor stores—10% of gross sales, plus liquor license and inventory.

4. Retail store—Seldom get more than depreciated value of fixtures and equipment, plus inventory at cost. Only when the retail store has an unusually high profit picture will the market bring any extra for goodwill. Generally, this is because a buyer feels he can rent his own space where he wants it, and stock it with his preference of inventory.

5. Grocery store—Will usually sell for inventory and re-placement cost of fixtures, plus a nominal amount for goodwill (about $3,000 to $4,000). If the grocery nets $25,000 and up, the amount of goodwill increases to about $8,000 to $10,000. If the net profit is $50,000 or above, the seller can usually get about 50% of the net profit as goodwill.

6. Liquor stores—Generally a small store can get inventory, depreciated value of fixtures, and about 50% of the net profit as goodwill. A large liquor store with high volume and profit of $40,000 and up can get one year's net profit, inventory, and fixtures.

7. General business—This model can be used when the following conditions exist:

(a) All inventory is not salable.

(b) The equipment and leasehold improvements are worth less than their cost.

(c) Profits can be substantiated.

Where:

V	=	Value
I	=	Inventory
LI	=	Leasehold Improvements
Eq	=	Equipment
El,E2,E3	=	Earnings for 3 years

Then:

$$V = .80\ I + \frac{LI + Eq}{2} + \frac{El,E2,E3}{3}$$

Example:

Where:

I	=	$400
LI	=	$20,000
Eq	=	$25,000
El,E2,E3	=	$30,000

Then:

$$V = .80 \times \$400 + \frac{\$25,000 + \$30,000}{2} + \frac{\$30,000}{3}$$

$$V = \$32,820$$

8. Auto repair garages—After a minimum income for the owner-mechanic ($6,000 to $20,000), a multiplier of 2 times the tangible assets less any liabilities.

9. Insurance agencies—100% to 150% of the annual fees or commissions received, plus a separate value for the client list, working capital, and fixed assets.

10. Advertising agencies—The sale of advertising agencies often involves the use of one of two possible formulas. The first being the computation of a premium for goodwill based on 30% to 50% of the tangible assets of the business less any liabilities.

   The second formula is a multiplier of 8 to 12 applied

to typical historical monthly profits before income taxes but after provision for salaries to the owners. The market value of the tangible assets less any liabilities is added to this goodwill factor.

11. Auto wrecking yards—Should earn at least 20% to 25% profit before income taxes and after management. Then 2 times monthly sales plus market value of tangible assets.

12. Funeral homes—Market value of tangible net worth, plus a bonus of $500 to $1,000 for each burial based on a typical recent year.

13. Nursing homes—The value of real estate or a dollar figure based on the price per bed, multiplied times the number of beds.

14. Arts and crafts shops—The fair market value of fixtures and equipment, the inventory at cost, and a goodwill factor of 15% of the annual net.

15. Auto parts—The fair market value of fixtures and equipment at cost, and not over .25 of annual net income for goodwill plus the accounts receivables.

16. Auto dealer, new cars—Fair market value of the fixtures and equipment, parts and inventory at cost, amount the dealer has invested in his new car inventory above the factory flooring, and the used cars at the wholesale book value. Goodwill value of up to 50% of annual net earnings are allowed if earnings are at least 18% gross.

17. Auto dealer, used cars—There is absolutely no goodwill in a used car lot. Valued at wholesale book in the inventory only.

18. Barber shops and beauty shops—Valued at $900 to $1,200 per chair plus 10% to 25% of annual net.

19. Bakers, retail—Fair market value of the fixtures and equipment plus the inventory at cost and goodwill of up to 15% of the annual gross.

20. Beer distributors—Valued at the fair market value of the fixtures and equipment, inventory at cost, and goodwill up to 1.25 times the annual net profit.

21. Boat dealer and marina—Valued at the fair market value of the fixtures and equipment, inventory at cost, and 1 times the annual net profit.

22. Building material and lumber yards—The fair market value of fixtures and equipment, current wholesale value of all lumber inventory and other inventory at cost plus 95% of accounts receivables and from 10% to 75% of the annual net.

23. Camera, stereo, and record shops—Fair market value of fixtures and 10% to 15% of its annual net profit.

24. Clothing stores—Fair market value of the fixtures and equipment, inventory at cost and culled for obsolete items, and goodwill at 10% to 25% of annual net.

25. Drug stores—Valued at fair market value of fixtures and equipment, and inventory at cost plus 25% of the annual gross.

26. Florist—Valued at fair market value of fixtures and equipment and inventory at cost plus goodwill of 25% of the annual gross.

27. Furniture store—Valued at fair market value of fixtures and equipment and inventory at cost, less obsolete items and 10% of the annual gross.

28. Grocery stores and meat markets—valued at fair market value of fixtures and equipment plus inventory at cost. There is seldom any goodwill in these ventures.

29. Hardware stores—Fair market value of fixtures and equipment and inventory at cost, less obsolete items plus 20% of net income.

30. Hobby shops—Same as #29.

31. Music stores—Same as #29 plus 33% of annual net profit.

32. Pet store—Same as #29 plus 35% to 50% of annual net profit.

33. Printers—Same as #29 plus 35% to 50% of annual net profit.

34. Restaurants and lounges—Valued at 40% of the annual gross or 1 times the annual net plus the fair market value of the fixtures and equipment.

35. Janitorial maintenance companies—Valued at 1 times one month's gross billings plus the fair market value of the fixtures and equipment.

Business Values Derived from Industy-related Pricing Models Based on Methods Other than Sales and Profit

1. Day care centers—$500 to $1,000 per child currently enrolled.

2. Gas stations—$1,000 for each 10,000 gallons per month pumped, plus gas in ground.

3. Restaurants—Selling price should be X times the daily average number of patrons or number of seats in a fixed-seating establishment.

4. Legal practices—The economic value of tangible assets, such as furniture, fixtures, and law library, plus an employment contract with the buyers which can cover the goodwill aspect of the seller.

5. Newspapers and periodicals—A determination of the

price per unit on circulation. This will vary depending on the type of newspaper or periodical. One weekly might sell for $2.00 per unit of circulation, whereas another might command $10.00. Another method is a percentage of the advertising volume.

6. Motels—$12,300 to $14,600 per room, based on motel sales national average in 1978.

7. WG technique—Many business owners tend to use this method when pricing their business. Basically the owner makes a wild guess.

8. SWG technique—One method of determining a business value for the retiring owner is to figure the cost of living expenses he will need for the next ten years, or what it will cost him to go on a trip around the world. This is known as the sophisticated wild guess.

9. Cost plus losses—This method is often used by the business owner that is not making sufficient profits. He wants to sell his business for his cost plus all of his operating losses.

10. The 50% method—Asking price of the seller divided by 50% equals price offered.

BASIC APPRAISAL CONCEPTS AND DEFINITIONS

The following concepts and definitions are those that have been generally accepted and published by various appraisal authors and associations.

1. Standards of value.

General definition of value: That quality of a thing which is thought of as being more or less desirable, useful, estimatable, or important.

(a)   Economic value: That kind of value according to which a thing is capable of producing economic benefits for its owner or user.

Price, cost, and value: Although the three terms are closely related, they actually have different meanings. In many cases, the terms are often confused and used incorrectly as though they were interchangeable.

As for *value,* as stated above, the quality of a thing according to which it is thought of as being more or less desirable, useful, estimatable, or important.

Price, on the other hand, refers to the amount of some medium of exchange, frequently but not necessarily money, that is needed to acquire a thing.

The term *cost* refers to the amount of one or more commodities such as money, labor, or material that is needed or expended to create or acquire a thing. Of the three terms, *price* and *cost* are closely related and may sometimes be identical. For example, if I purchased something from a store, the sum of money that I pay is also the price the store receives for the merchandise and is also my cost of acquiring it. However, it is generally not the same as the store's cost of acquiring the article in the first place.

Kinds of economic value:

(i)   Book value: The value of an asset or group of assets (including a complete business) as stated on the owner's financial statements or accounting records. This value frequently differs from other types of value for reasons such as tax considerations.

(ii)   Fair market value (market value): One common definition that is especially useful for appraisal purposes is that fair market value is the price, in cash or equivalent, that a buyer could reasonably be expected to pay and a seller could reasonably be expected to accept, if the property were exposed for sale on the open market for a reasonable period of time, both buyer and seller being in possession of the pertinent facts, and neither being under compulsion to act.

(iii)　Fair value: To understand what the expression *fair value* means, you have to know the context of its use. In business appraisal, the term *fair value* is a legally created standard of value that applies to certain specific transactions.

In most states, fair value is the statutory standard of value applicable in cases of dissenting stockholders' appraisal rights. In most states, if a corporation merges, sells out, or takes certain other actions, and the owner of a minority interest believes that he is being forced to receive less than adequate consideration for his stock, he has the right to have his shares appraised and to receive fair value in cash. In states that have adopted the Uniform Business Corporation Act, the definition of fair value is as follows: *Fair value*, with respect to dissenter's shares, means the value of the shares immediately before the effectuation of the corporate action to which the dissenter objects, excluding any appreciation or depreciation in anticipation of the corporate action unless exclusion would be inequitable.

(iv)　Going concern value: Value of a business considered as an operating enterprise rather than as merely a collection of assets and liabilities.

The term may be useful to refer either to the total value of a going concern or to that portion of the total value that exceeds the value of the other identifiable assets of the business.

(v)   Goodwill value:

(1) Value attributable to goodwill.

(2) The value of the advantages that a business has developed as a result of intangibles applicable to the specific business itself, such as name, reputation, and so on.

(3) That part of the total value of a going enterprise that is in excess of the capital investment; an ingredient of *going concern value.*

(vi)   Insurable value: That portion of the value of an asset or asset group that is acknowledged or recognized under the provisions of an applicable loss insurance policy.

(vii)   Investment value:

(1) Value as determined or estimated in accordance with the investment value (income) approach.

(2) The value of a thing that arises from its presumed ability to produce a profit or return on investment for its owner.

(3) Value to a particular investor based upon individual investment requirements as distinguished from market value which is value to a broader market than a single investor.

(viii)   Liquidation value: The (estimated) proceeds, net after provisions for applicable liabilities, if any, that would result from the sale of an asset or a group of assets, if sold individually and not as part of the business enterprise of which they were originally a part. Sale may involve either forced liquidation or orderly disposal, with the amount of the net proceeds likely different for the two situations.

(ix) Present Value: In investment theory, the current monetary value, frequently in the sense of the current value of future benefits. Discounted value of aggregate future payments.

(x) Replacement value:

(1) The value of a business, asset, or asset group, as determined by the replacement cost approach.

(2) Value as determined on the basis of the estimated cost of replacing the assets in question with other items of like kind and condition, and capable of producing equivalent benefits (results) for the user. Replacement value can be either depreciated replacement value or replacement value new.

(b) Other kinds of value:

Religious value	Social value
Sentimental value	Ethical value
Philosophical value	Moral value

2. Principles of appraising:

(a) Principle of substitution: The value of a thing tends to be determined by the cost of acquiring an equally desirable substitute.

(i) Universe of equally desirable substitutes: An *equally desirable substitute* may take on a somewhat different meaning, and the search for such substitutes as a basis for comparison will not necessarily be limited to other property of similar kind, function, or geographic location.

(b) Principle of alternatives: In any contemplated transaction, each party has alternatives to consummating a transaction.

Alternatives can:

(i)   Buy another existing similar business.

(ii) Start an equivalent business from scratch.

(iii) Make an investment in some completely different type investment.

(iv) And most frequently do nothing.

(c) Principle of future benefits: Economic value reflects anticipated future benefits. Justice Oliver Wendell Holmes said, "All values are anticipations of the future." No one buys a business simply because of what it has accomplished in the past, or even what it consists of at present. Although past performance and present status can offer important insight to what the business is likely to do in the future, it is the anticipated future performance of a business that gives it economic value.

STEPS IN THE APPRAISAL PROCESS

1. Defining the appraisal assignment: In this first and most important process the first step is to define exactly what it is you are valuing and for what the report will be used. It is obvious, that this is not only the most important step,

but also should define the type of report needed. Therefore, it is important to determine:

(a) Purpose and function of an appraisal:

    (i) Purpose—Type of value to be estimated, e.g., fair market value or other.

    (ii) Function—Use of the appraisal results.

2. Defining value to be estimated: Once you have determined the type of value that will be the basis of your report and what will be the function, then equally important is to define the property to be appraised and as of what date in time.

    There are several things to consider:

(a) Are you valuing the entire corporation, that will include the corporate stock, or only a certain block of shares, or is the company a proprietorship or partnership?

(b) Are all of the assets of the company to be valued? If not which ones?

(c) Are all liabilities to be valued and if so, which ones?

(d) What is the effective value date of the valuation?

3. Gathering the pertinent facts:

    Internal information about the business: Internal information about the business will usually be in the form of financial statements or income tax returns on the subject business and interviews with persons who are acquainted with some or all aspects of the business, as well as the appraiser's personal observation of the business. This should be a close observation of its facilities and the condition of the equipment. As we discussed earlier, it is important to ask questions about the equipment, its age, condition, and date of last rebuild. It is also wise, if available, to obtain a copy of the maintenance records. Inquire about the capacity of the equipment and physical plant. As discussed earlier, if the company is growing and from your research you determine that the company should continue to grow, at what capacity level must new capital equipment be purchased? You must consider this in projecting future growth and profits. If the company is of the type that may have environmental consequences, now is the time to inspect all aspects and records pertaining to this issue until you are satisfied that you have done a thorough inspection with regards to environmental issues.

General information: There are numerous aspects of the company that need to be researched in order to make the assumptions that will be addressed in the various valuation methods.

Remember the importance of future anticipations regarding the continued growth of the company. The following items of research on your part will give you a perception of the future or will confuse you. Either result is important because what you are doing is looking at the company and hopefully will see and feel what the potential buyer feels. Always remember this feeling of either certainty or uncertainty is the basis for almost all of the mathematical calculation decisions in the various methods and formulas. If after your research on the business you feel certain of its continued success, this equates to a lower risk factor and thus a higher value. If you are uncertain or confused about the future success of the company, this is how a buyer will view it. This perception of uncertainty makes the buyer uncomfortable and he perceives the business as risky, requiring a higher return in order to purchase it at a lower price. It is extremely important to understand that as the appraiser, you are like a newspaper reporter, you only report the news. You do not make it. Another example is that you are the thermometer, not the thermostat.

Naturally, very few companies are alike and there is no perfect set of guidelines that can be used to research all companies. However, the following topics should be researched on all companies.

(a) Products and/or services: Many appraisers will simply bypass any research on products or services, assuming they will stay status quo. However, we have encountered many instances where the subject company's main ingredient or component was to increase dramatically in the coming year. In one instance, the main supplier for raw materials was in bankruptcy and although the materials could be purchased elsewhere if they did not recover, there was no guarantee that the costs would remain the same and therefore projections, at best, were a guess. Remember, uncertainty relates to risk and risk relates to value. We found other problems with companies relating to their service. Although sales seemed to be stable from past performance, some of the customers were not going to renew their contract when due in three to six months. Another case of this was a major competitor moved into the area and had already decreased volume by 25% in the past quarter, which conveniently was withheld from us because the owner said his accountant was swamped during tax season and they had to file an extension.

(b) Existing lines: Is the company going to be able to keep the existing lines from a distributor? Has the distributer signed an exclusive territory agreement with the company or can they assign new distributors in the subject company's trade area?

(c) Opportunities for related lines: Can the company pick up other lines that could be sold to the same customer with no increase in marketing? How much would this add to the bottom line?

(d) Patents, copyrights, trademarks: Patents, copyrights, and trademarks may have value over and above the price of the business. This can be a whole new valuation. One of the keys to having a seperate value is if the patent, copyright, or trademark could be sold on its own as a separate entity. In most cases these assets are what gives the company its profitability and security and are usually valued as an allocation of the goodwill value. Security relates to risk, therefore, the more secure, the less risk, and the company enjoys a higher value.

However this is not by any means the norm for dealing with these types of assets. This is an area where you must really be careful and understand what you are doing.

(e) Relative profitability of lines: Take a good look at each of the product lines that the company handles and research the likelihood of its longevity. In looking at some of the product lines separately, you may find that the hottest-selling product produces the least amount of profit and that profit has been going down for some time. Also, does the company have a secure contract to market this product line for years to come? If the company manufactures this product line, will there be any likely increases in raw materials that will effect its profitability in the coming years?

Are there any warranties included with or purchased separately with the company's product and what has been the historical cost of this? If the product line is increasing, at what capacity will new equipment have to be installed to keep up with orders and in what condition is the present equipment that produces this product?

(f) Markets and marketing: What is the market like for this product, is it a fad or will it continue for years to come?

Are there any major technological breakthroughs with production or equipment which will cause the company to be uncompetitive in the future?

(g) Market reputation

(h) Geographic scope

(i) Method of marketing and distribution

(j) Pricing policies

(k) Customer base

(l) Customer relations

(m) Market continuity, growth opportunities, and weaknesses

(n) Supplier relationships:

    (i) Continuity

    (ii) Degree of exclusivity

    (iii) Contractual relationships

    (iv) Supplier restrictions

(o) Physical facilities:

    (i) Adequacy of facility

    (ii) Condition

    (iii) Plant (size, owned or rented, etc.)

        (iv)   Equipment (kinds, age, values, etc.)

(p) Management and employees:

        (i)   Size and composition of workforce

        (ii)   Key employees

        (iii)   Other employees

        (iv)   Compensation

        (v)   Personnel policies, satisfaction, conflict, and turnover

        (vi)   How does the company get new employees?

(q) Operating efficiencies and inefficiencies:

        (i)   Physical plant

        (ii)   Accounting and other controls

(r) General outlook for business

(s) Pending litigation

(t) Reason for sale

(u) Financial information:

        (i)   Past financial performance of the business

        (ii)   Income/expense (profit) information

        (iii)   Trends

        (iv)   Present financial status of the business

        (v)   Balance sheet (asset and liability information)

(v) External information about the business:

        (i)   Local and regional information

        (ii)   Labor supply

        (iii)   Employment/unemployment

        (iv)   Material availability

        (v)   Taxes

        (vi)   Local and regional growth trends

(vii)   Industry information

(viii) Competition and potential for future competition

(ix)   General outlook for the industry

(x)   Markets and channels of distribution

(xi)   Special industry situations that may affect the business either positively or negatively

(xii)   Present regulation

(xiii) Potential changes in regulatory environment

(xiv) Effect of technological developments

4. Analyzing the facts: Once you have gathered both the internal and external information about the company, you must now use your research results in the assumptions that affect the various formulas in the methods you will use to arrive at a final conclusion of value.

5. Three approaches to value: There are three basic approaches to appraising real, personal, tangible, and intangible property. They are the cost approach, market comparable approach, and income approach. Within each approach there are numerous methods used to determine value. An appraisal should include a review of each approach.

   (a) Cost approach: The cost approach is to determine the total asset value of the business. These methods can consist of the reproduction value (exact), otherwise known as the cost-to-create method, the replacement value (similar), in-place market value (economic depreciation/used), liquidation value (forced or orderly disposition), or book value.

       The Internal Revenue Service has divided the types of assets into four categories:

Class I assets

Cash and deposits in bank

Class II assets

Certificates of deposits, U.S. government securities, marketable stocks, foreign currency.

Class III assets

Inventory, accounts receivables, fixed assets, real estate.

Class IV assets

Intangibles

(b) Market comparable approach: Comparison of the subject property to other similar properties is the essence of the market comparable approach. The single most important market factor to impact the value of a business is the supply and demand of an equally desirable substitute that is available in the market place.

According to the principle of substitution, the value of a thing (business) tends to be determined by the cost of acquiring an equally desirable substitute. The concept of valuation considering an equally desirable substitute dictates that a buyer will pay no more for a business than what he or she can currently purchase the same or another business of like kind. This concept is the basis of fair market value and is the overriding methodology in this chapter.

There are only three approaches to determining the value of any asset; the cost approach, which basically considers the cost of purchasing or producing the business, the market comparable approach which values the business based on current sales in the market place for the same or similar business, and the income approach which is a mathematical analysis of capitalizing an income stream by a return that best represents the activity of the current market.

In other types of valuations, mainly real estate, the market comparable approach indisputably will always yield the most accurate results. It is a true representation of the current marketplace because it is what the market is paying for the same or similar asset. However, as stated earlier, in the case of a business, using public or private comparable sales price-to-earnings or income-to-sales ratios may be the least reliable for several reasons. No two businesses are alike, business sales are not recorded and therefore information gathered is usually sketchy. Accounting records are not always standard between the same companies, there is no standard definition of *net profit* or *income, revenue, cost of sales* and many others. Some comparable sales include assets that the subject business does not have and these assets are not valued separately, therefore the appraiser cannot make proper adjustments. The market data approach can be very useful when analyzing data drawn from the market as to what types of return on investment or data based on multiples of annual earnings that buyers are willing to pay in order to purchase a certain type of business.

It can be argued that the use of stock prices of publicly owned companies to estimate the market value of privately held companies is a source of comparable data. However, most business appraisers realize that to estimate the market value of a privately held business using this data is seriously flawed in several respects:

(i) Publicly held companies whose stocks are listed on the major exchanges are usually much larger than closely held businesses that are being appraised. This difference in size raises serious questions as to whether the two are, in fact comparable.

(ii) Prices of publicly traded stock always reflect the sale of a very small fraction of ownership interests. On the other hand, the appraiser's objective is usually to estimate the market value of a major ownership interest, frequently 100% ownership of the closely held business.

(iii) The above must be selected by the appraiser through a process that amounts to little more than guesswork, and thus cannot be relied upon.

(iv) The price-to-earnings ratio represents the ratio of a current stock to an earnings-per-share figure that can be from a few weeks to several months old.

(v) Probably the greatest fallacy of attempting to use publicly traded stock prices to estimate the value of a closely held business lies in the psychology of the investor.

   The potential buyer for a closely held business is almost always concerned with the anticipated performance of the business itself. Of course, it is sometimes argued that the trend of stock prices of publicly held companies is strongly influenced by the industry's performance. However, it is demonstrable that, whereas this does tend to be true in the long run, there are many influences on stock that tend to be of short-term nature, and that strongly influence stock prices while bearing relatively little long-term relationship to the company's fortunes. This is not usually recommended as a means of estimating the value of closely held businesses.

(vi) Still another source of market data is information on actual sales of companies, such as the subject, in the appraiser's local community. It is unlikely, however, that there will be enough information available on sales similar to the subject to provide a statistically sound basis for estimating market value.

In conclusion, on the subject of the market data approach for closely held businesses, while we may sometimes include information or make comments on similar business sales that might have reciprocity in valuation techniques, the lack of enough market data from public or private sales, based solely on price-to-earnings and income to selling price may make this technique unsound and may eliminate the use of the market data approach.

In the cost approach, the cost of an item is rarely what its selling price or value may be and, in many cases, price is not the value. This is especially true in a rapidly changing market which is highly affected by technological changes or variances in supply and demand or a company that is very strong but has not yet established enough longevity to make a confident analysis of the fixture performance.

In the case of a business, all serious practitioners of business valuation agree that book value is not necessarily an adequate proxy for representing the underlying net asset for valuation purposes, much less for representing the value of the business itself. However, book value is a figure that is available for almost all businesses. Furthermore, it is a value that different businesses have arrived at by some more or less common set of rules, usually some variation within the scope of generally accepted accounting principles (GAAP). Also, each asset or liability number that is a component of book value as shown in the financial statements represents a specific set of obligations that can be identified in detail by referring to the company's records, assuming that the bookkeeping is complete and accurate.

Therefore, book value usually provides the most convenient starting point for an asset value approach to the valuation of a business interest.

The nature and extent of adjustments that should be made to book value for the business valuation depend on many factors. One, of course, is the valuation's purpose. Another which is frequently a limiting factor, is the availability of reliable data on which to base the adjustments both for the subject company and for other companies which might be compared in the course of the valuation. Another concept for fixed assets is *value in use*, the value of the operating assets to the owner/user or buyer who will use them in a similar manner. This value includes consideration for the unique relationship of the item to a particular business such as the subject.

There is a value for an item which is already in place and is ready to use. The value might be the item's retail price, plus applicable taxes, freight, and installation charges. The summation of these costs, after proper deductions for depreciation and obsolescence, is the *value in use* of that item. This value may be different from its *fair market value* to the buyer who will not use the equipment at its present location.

(c)   Income approach:

The income approach considers a business as though it were a money machine whose purpose is to produce money for its owners. This approach best encompasses the principle of substitution, that is, the value of a thing tends to be determined by the cost of acquiring an equally desirable substitute.

This method involves estimating the amount of future income that will be produced by a business, then determines the applicable relationships between income and value, and then converts the income into an opinion of value.

The income approach is especially meaningful if the assets are used to produce income, such as in the valuation of a business. However, it still takes root from the market data approach because it is an analysis of what the current market is paying by determining a comparable return that can be capitalized into a comparable purchase price.

SOURCES OF INFORMATION

1. Economic information sources
   (a) National economy
       (i)   Statistical sources
           (1) Standard and Poor's statistical services
               Security prices index
               Current statistics
           (2) *The Federal Reserve Bulletin*
           (3) *The Statistical Abstract of the United States*
       (ii)   Business periodicals
           (1) *Fortune*
           (2) *Forbes*
           (3) *Business Week*
           (4) *Dun's Business Week*
           (5) *The Wall Street Journal*
       (iii) Inflation forecasts
           (1) *Fortune*
           (2) *Standard & Poor's Trends and Projections*
           (3) *Predicasts forecasts*
       (iv) Banks
       (v)   Monetary policy, fiscal policy, and the political environment
           (1) Business periodicals
           (2) Federal reserve district banks
   (b) Regional economy
       (i)   Banks

(ii)   State and local business magazines and newspapers

(iii)   State and city government offices

   (1) Employment divisions

   (2) Chambers of Commerce

2.   Industry information sources

  (a)   General business periodicals/publications

    (i)   National business periodicals

      (1) Use indexes such as:

        Predicasts Index of Corporations and Industries

        Business periodicals index

      (2) Annual industry outlooks published by:

        Forbes

        Fortune

        Business Week

    (ii)   Sales and Marketing Management's Annual Survey of Buying Power Magazine

    (iii)   *Standard & Poor's Industry Surveys*

  (b)   Industry Financial Data

    (i)   *Robert Morris Associates Annual Statement Studies*

    (ii)   *Financial Research Associates*

    (iii)   *Dun and Bradstreet's Key Business Ratios*

    (iv)   *Standard and Poor's Analyst Handbook*

  (c)   Trade associations

    (i)   The National Trade and Professional Association of the United States (NPTA) is useful as a directory

(d) Trade magazines

    (i) Business publications rates and data is useful as an index

(e) Government publications

    (i) *U.S. Industrial Outlook*

    (ii) Other

(f) Banks

2

MARKETING BUSINESS VALUATIONS

(A Step-by-Step Marketing Process for Professionals Offering These Services)

EVERY BUYER AND SELLER NEEDS A VALUATION!

Some successful persons in sales promote the idea that the best way to sell something is to not sell it, especially if the need is as obvious as a business valuation. This *soft sell* or *reverse* approach is often effective in marketing valuations. Many times I use some of the following comments when I am face-to-face with a business owner who is contemplating placing a business on the market.

"The obvious first step in selling a business is to do a professional business valuation. In order to get that started, I need the following initial information . . ."

"After many years of assisting owners in the sales of businesses, I must give you the same advice you would probably receive from your attorney, accountant, banker, or even your uncle: Don't do anything until you have a valuation performed to determine you are not leaving money on the table."

"You should never consider selling anything of great value, especially a business in which you have invested many years, without first having a valuation performed. In fact, you would not even consider selling a used car without researching the potential price in a NADA book."

"Selling your business is one of the most important steps you take in a lifetime. I should tell you those I've observed to be the most successful always start with a professional business valuation."

"I can't imagine any professional you use (attorney, accountant, banker, etc.) who would not advise you to first secure a professional valuation."

"There are several important steps involved in the successful sale of a business. Any professional would probably tell you the first is to secure a professional business valuation."

"Experience tells us those who usually get the best price for their business secure a professional business valuation to back up their price."

"I have observed more sellers underprice their business than overprice it. Consequently, I don't think I want to participate unless we do a valuation. I don't want a phone call from you in a year or so complaining we sold it too cheap."

"The common thread I see running through all business sales is that the successful ones started with a professional business valuation. I'm sure you can understand why I don't want to participate in the marketing of your business unless we start with one!"

Comments like these set an attitude from the beginning: we are going to do things right and the first right thing to do is a professional business valuation. Anything less is really not appropriate and should not be considered by anyone who is serious about selling their business. Even though anyone performing a valuation must be paid for doing so, it should not be looked at as a cost, but rather a way to maximize value. A proper business valuation saves money in the negotiation process, and in fact, makes money in supporting a maximum price and better terms because it demonstrates that the seller is asking fair market price.

If a potential seller is not willing to invest in a valuation to properly price a business, it should be obvious they are not serious about selling and therefore not worthy of consuming the time and efforts of others.

To sell business valuations you must believe in these statements and be willing to walk away from an assignment if the seller is not willing to invest in a valuation. This report makes sellers and buyers *informed decision makers.*

OTHER EVENTS THAT REQUIRE VALUATIONS

Buying and selling businesses are not the only activities that trigger the need for a professional business valuation. The business valuation is a *decision-making document.* The facts in the report provide the necessary information to make a decision to do many things. Many other events require an independent third-party valuation:

- Mergers
- Loan applications
- Preparation for legal representation
- Family succession
- Estate planning
- Divorce proceedings
- Future growth planning

- Industry standards comparison
- Partnership disputes
- Annual partnership or corporation requirements
- Tax purposes

THERE IS A NEED TO MARKET THESE SERVICES

Even though most professionals and principals involved in business activities agree on the need for business valuations, *do not assume* they will all think of calling you and ordering one every time there is a potential need. Actually, you should not assume they agree on the need. Like any other professional service, you must first sell yourself, sell the need for your service, and then provide the service at a higher standard than anyone anticipated.

Anyone in this industry who assumes all the business they can handle will come to them just because they are available, will soon find this arrogant attitude abruptly removing them from the industry! We live and work in a competitive, global society with the need to upgrade, justify, and market our services on a regular basis.

In marketing valuations, you must first make a definite personal commitment to tell everyone with whom you communicate about offering the "most widely used and economical business valuations in the industry." This will become a consistent part of all your verbal and written business communications. Add this to your stationary, cards, brochures, and all advertising (see Exhibit 2.1 for other sample marketing phrases). At the end of this chapter in Exhibit 2.2 you will find a sample press release you should immediately send to all newspapers, professional publications, radio and TV stations, and so on. You will also find a sample form letter in Exhibit 2.3 you should customize and send to every currently known individual for whom you have previously provided services.

Marketing your valuation services will not only bring new valuation clients, it will also attract more users of the other services you offer. This makes it imperative that you develop a consistent, weekly marketing plan to reach those for whom you do not now provide a service or with whom you do not normally communicate.

DEFINE YOUR MARKETING STRATEGIES

1. Select your marketing area. To define the geographical area where you will work, first secure a list of all businesses in an easy driving distance of your current office. I suggest you begin marketing businesses with 5 or more employees. These lists are almost always available from the local professional societies or chamber of commerce, and can be purchased from American Business Directories, Dun & Bradstreet, and many others. Beginning with zip codes contiguous with your office and working outward, assemble the prospects in the area in which you want to work.

2. Organize the area for prospecting activities. Beginning with your office zip code, organize the prospects closest to your office as follows:

   Group 1: Businesses with 50 or more employees

   Group 2: Businesses with 20 to 49 employees

   Group 3: Businesses with 10 to 19 employees

   Group 4: Businesses with 5 to 9 employees

Using the businesses with the largest number of employees first, put these in mailing groups of 25 businesses.

3. Make preparation for prospect mailings. Decide if you
   will use mailing labels or if you will have each letter per-
   sonalized through your word processing system with each
   prospect name and address on each letter and envelope.
   The latter is more successful! Enter the first 25 prospects
   into your word processing system or prepare (or purchase)
   the mailing labels.

4. Prospect mailings. Prepare 25 prospect letters (example
   provided in Exhibit 2.3 at the end of this chapter). Include your calling card, enclose in envelopes, stamp, and
   mail on Wednesday.

5. Prospect telephone calls for appointments. On Tuesday,
   following the mailing on Wednesday, begin calling the
   prospects using the prospect telephone script (example
   provided in Exhibit 2.4 at the end of this chapter).

6. Prospect presentation preparations. Prepare a professional
   presentation notebook for use in your presentations. Have
   an adequate supply of the following:

   Your company brochure

   Your calling cards

   Your personal copy of a sample business valuation you
      have done previously

   (If available, have a sample of the industry of the pros-
      pect)

7. Prospect presentation. Use of your professional presentation notebook and/or outline is suggested, however,
   some feel comfortable with a casual conversation approach even though they still follow the outline by
   memory and use the presentation pages as appropriate.

8. Order/agreement for performance of business valuation. You should prepare a form which will serve as the official agreement between you (and/or the independent third party) and the client that spells out the normal understandings between the parties. Collect the entire amount from the person ordering from you at the time of their order. Your decisions are your business. However, it is easier to collect the total amount when the valuations are ordered!

9. Delivery of the business valuation. Most professionals selling valuation reports prepare two copies for the client and want the opportunity to personally deliver the valuations.

10. Opportunity for other services. Many of the valuations will be ordered by clients who are anticipating selling or buying a business. You should know the motivation of your client and follow up accordingly.

WHO SHOULD PERFORM BUSINESS VALUATIONS?

Who should perform business valuations and what is the reality check regarding potential litigation are questions often asked by those entering the industry. Those entering anything new must deal with the fact of competition from others with more experience. However, everyone must start somewhere and the need for proper education and certification is a legitimate concern for all.

Adequate understanding of this volume is the best start you can find, but not the end of the journey. A good next step could be the purchase of a computer program prepared by someone who has been highly regarded in the industry for many years. The proper use of a computer program will guide you through the accepted steps of the industry and make it more difficult to make common mistakes. This also gives you some immediate credibility, with the end result being a much more professional presentation.

A recent survey of professionals offering business valuations revealed some of them ultimately require justification in front of an opposing attorney in a courtroom. In an effort to discredit the person providing the valuation, we found the following questions often used in the presence of the judge and/or jury:

"How many business valuations did you do in the last two years?"

"How many have you done on similar businesses in the last two years?"

"What business valuation courses have you taken?"

"What were they?"

"Describe what was covered in detail."

"What valuation and/or appraisal designations do you have and what was required to receive them?"

"What is required to retain them?"

"What methodology(s) do you use and what alternative methods did you consider?"

"What articles and/or books have you written about business valuation?"

"What percentage of your time is spent in business valuations?"

"Does your report follow IRS revenue guidelines?"

"How did you arrive at the type of market value to be used?"

"Why do you feel it is appropriate?"

"Where do you get your comparables?"

"Have you followed the departure provisions or does your report meet the standards as set by the Appraisal Foundation, as required by law under the Uniform Standards of Professional Appraisal Practice (USPAP)?"

"Have you ever worked for this client before and in what capacity?"

"By what professional practices do you claim this to be unbiased?"

Providing the above information is not an attempt to alarm you, but to adequately prepare you for the eventual need to justify your work.

INDEPENDENT THIRD-PARTY VALUATIONS

Buyers and sellers often need more than a broker or an intermediary. Regardless of the professional title you use, they may need a counselor to perform or coordinate the performing of other requirements. Secure more training and certifications in order to be qualified to meet their needs with flexibility. I saw a sign in a retail establishment recently:

"If we don't meet the needs of the customer, someone else will, and they'll take away our business in the process!"

Even though specialization is a buzzword in the industry (or at least it used to be), a single approach to working with sellers and buyers is becoming unrealistic.

I have seen many professionals entering the field find a great source of income to be the marketing of valuations during their time of study and preparations. They deal with the client face-to-face, gather all of the needed information which is used by a third-party with all the credentials and experience who provides the actual report. The fees collected for the service are shared on a compatible basis. In fact, I have seen this work so well for some, they permanately use the team approach and find both earning more money for their efforts. ABC (Alliance of Business Consultants) is a national organization of accountants and attorneys, most of whom use this approach on a regular basis. Other professional associations such as the IBBA (International Business Brokers Association), CBC (Certified Business Counselors), ASA (the American Society of Appraisers), and IBA (Institute of Business Appraisers) offer business valuation training and network opportunities. Many intermediaries feel it is much easier to sell valuations performed by an independent third-party because they:

1. Are more believable to potential buyers and the professionals they use.

2. Reduce the liability of the selling professional not preparing the report.

3. The potential negative result does not interfere with the relationship between the selling professional not preparing the report and their seller or buyer.

4. Provide a greater comfort level to the seller or buyer in receiving a credible report from someone who has nothing else to gain from the action.

5. Hopefully avoid the automatic reduction of 20% or more when the report comes from someone already associated with the seller.

6. Help the seller to feel more comfortable about not leaving money on the table.

7. More impressive to the IRS, who wants to see the allocation of assets after the sale.

8. Make a buyer more willing to make better offers quickly because they know the seller is serious and is only seeking a fair price.

9. Eliminates quickly the "buyer in the wing," claimed by the seller.

Personally, I have a policy of not performing the valuation when I am serving the buyer or seller in any other capacity. I think it is more professional to use the team approach! You will find many other professionals who believe in the team approach and will be glad to refer valuation clients to you. Business owners, sellers, and buyers who know and respect you will also be great sources of referrals. Use this as another opportunity to increase your circle of influence as a professional. The industry is experiencing a phenomenal growth because of an enormous need for professional business valuations. Whatever your approach, find your niche, and regularly participate in educational opportunities! Check the addresses in the Industry Resource Lists section and contact some of the above-referenced professional associations.

Exhibit 2.1

Sample Marketing Phrases

Verbal and Written

Verbal: Without exception, you should include a version of the following phrases the first time you verbally communicate with any current or prospective client:

"Did you know I now offer* _____ services? Do you currently need, or know of anyone who needs these services?

Written: Without exception, you should include a version of the following phrases the first time you communicate in a written form with any current or prospective client:

"I (our firm) now offer(s) * _____ services! Please give me (us) a call when you, or anyone you know, needs these services!"

Stationery, Cards, and Brochures: You may add the fact that you offer * _____ services to these printed materials.

Certifications/Designations: As you achieve them, you should add these certifications and designations to all printed materials *only after* you have successfully completed all requirements. They are to follow your name, such as:

William W. (Bill) Bumstead,
CBC, FCBI, BCB, LREB, PBC, LPI

*The services you offer.

Exhibit 2.2

Sample Press Release

Offers Business Evaluation Services

_____ (your firm) has announced the appointment of _____ as a specialist in business valuations. In announcing the appointment, _____ stressed that _____ not only adheres to a strict code of ethics, but has additional training and knowledge in business, taxation, and law, commits to stringent training requirements, and will participate in continuing education. He/she also participates in a networking system and referral base of knowledgeable and professional members who understand and can advise in all aspects surrounding the business valuation industry. Here are a few times when you may need business valuation services: _Selling a Business, Buying a Business, Tax Purposes, Loan Applications, Preparation for Legal Representation, Family Succession, Estate Planning, Divorce Proceedings, Future Growth Planning, Industry Comparison, Partnership Disputes, Annual Partnership/Corporation Requirements,_ etc.

_____ is a ____ year old company in the _____ profession. _____ stressed the fact they are extremely proud to announce the appointment of _____ as a specialist in business valuations. _____ may be reached at (___) ___-____, with offices at _____ .

Exhibit 2.3

Sample Form Letter

Date

Joe Prospect
Prospects, Inc.
1234 Colorado Ave.
Denver, CO 80002

Dear Joe:

What Is Your Business Worth?

A recent survey of business owners revealed one of their greatest concerns to be the true value of their greatest single asset, their business. In fact, many who had made an effort to determine what their business was worth had undervalued it rather than overvaluing it.

Since your business is probably your most important investment, it is important to have its current value assessed at least *every two years* in order to determine the progress you are making on ultimate goals. Some partnership and corporate agreements require this *annually.*

Those considering the sale or purchase of a business normally consider this to be the first step before entering into any marketing or negotiating activities. Common sense dictates a valuation by someone with specific training and experience in business valuations. This makes the results more acceptable to all parties involved.

Other events that create the need for an independent business evaluation often include:

Family succession	Estate planning
Divorce proceedings	Tax purposes
Partnership disputes	Future growth plans
Loan applications	Industry standards comparison
Preparation for legal representation	

In our area many of the better buyers of businesses come from other states. It's easy to see why others want to live here and will often pay more to do so! This is why it is essential that your business valuation be performed with our experience, data, and contacts.

We would appreciate having the opportunity to introduce you to our valuation and appraisal system, the *most widely used and economical in the industry.* It does not cost any more to get the best, why settle for less? Please call me at (___) ___-____ for a free confidential consultation!

Sincerely,

(Your name and certifications)

Exhibit 2.4

Business Valuation Prospect Telephone Script

(When Talking on the Telephone . . . Talk Slow in a Conversational Tone!)

Hi, this is _____ . I'm calling to follow up on a letter mailed to you regarding the need for business valuations.

Do you have a minute?

As explained in the letter:

Business owners need to keep current on the value of their business with an update at least *every two years.*

Some partnership and corporate agreements require an *annual* business evaluation. Can you believe that many of them think it is worth *less* than the real market value? If you have had any thoughts of selling, you can understand why it is important to use a properly trained professional to do the valuation. This makes the results more acceptable to all parties involved.

(continued)

Exhibit 2.4 (continued)

In the letter there was a list of nine events that usually trigger the need for a valuation. Are you contemplating any of these, like a:

Family succession   Estate planning
Divorce proceedings   Tax purposes
Partnership disputes   Future growth plans
Loan applications   Industry standards comparison
Preparation for legal representation

We really live in a global marketplace. Even though you may operate locally, the value of your business is better determined by standards from all across the nation. Some buyers from other states will pay more. This is why it is essential that your business valuation be performed with our expertise, data, and contacts. It really does not cost any more to get the best.

May I have the opportunity to come share with you the *most widely used and economical business valuation system* in the world? This will be a free and totally confidential consultation in your office!

Would _____ @ _____ or _____ @ _____ be better for you?

Fine, I can meet with you on: _____ @ _____ ?

I'm looking forward to meeting in your office on: _____ @ _____ . Be sure to mark it on your calendar!

If they ask "what does it cost?", answer with:

The meeting in your *office* costs nothing.

The price for a valuation will be determined by your needs; however, our prices are running below the local market.

3

DON'T WRESTLE WITH PORCUPINES

(Helping Professionals Avoid Pitfalls in the Industry)

I grew up in the country in deep east Texas, where most male family recreation was found in hunting, fishing, and other similar activities. My dad, brother, and I learned some real lessons for life and one of them was to not *wrestle with porcupines*. In case you've not been personally introduced to one, they are a rather large rodent type animal, covered with very sharp, long quills. Dad worked out of town and a lot of our outdoor activities took place at night after he came home from work. One night the Bumstead Boys were out on our forty acres which seemed like thousands of acres, especially at night to a youngster in elementary school. Dad always had good hunting dogs who would be out in front of us looking for the scent of the prey of the night. On this particular night, the harmonious howling and barking in front of us got our adrenaline and brisk steps moving forward in anticipation until we found both dogs frantically digging at a hole in the side of a hill. Ammunition cost money and we were taught not to shoot at just anything. It was decision time, do you find out what is in the hole or do you move on? In order to impress my older brother and dad, I volunteered to put my hand in the hole to be sure we were not leaving something important. Before I could hear the advice of my brother and dad, I had reached in and grabbed more than I had anticipated. You guessed it, it was a very upset porcupine whose quills immediately went to work on me. I can well remember my dad saying, "Get rid of it son, it's not a matter of whether you are going to get stuck, it's a matter of how long you are going to hold on and how much pain you want to endure."

His advice has served me well in this industry when it has been time to learn lessons without having to repeat the same mistakes. After being stuck more than once on the same issues, I would like to warn business valuation and intermediary professionals about some pitfalls in this industry that will leave real deep quill marks in your pride and pocketbook. If you don't avoid these little monsters, it's not a matter of whether you are going to get stuck, it's a matter of how much pain you want to endure and how much money you want to lose in the process.

The first porcupine concerns the warning that business valuation and intermediary professionals should not depend entirely on the anticipation of large commissions that are earned by some in the industry! Selling businesses is still mostly a commission-structured career and if you are not earning a significant part of your income from these justified fees you may not be adequately serving those sellers and buyers who have placed their trust in you. Your interest in this industry possibly came from some of the volumes of success stories that prove the proper combination of events can make your commission visions become a reality. These are the dreams that help us achieve our highest level of performance. My experience and observation reveal hard facts regarding the inconsistent timing of the receipt of commissions, which does not necessarily coincide with the consistent expenses necessary to serve those who use your professional services.

PORCUPINES ARE INEVITABLE IN THIS BUSINESS!

At best, professionals serving buyers and sellers of businesses are going to have to handle a few of them, so why not get paid for it? It is necessary that you train those who use your services to pay for them as they receive them and some of that is up front! Don't give away your services; charge for everything you do and get paid as you do it! One very pleasant memory reminds me of the bright side of the subject of collecting fees. About 15 years ago I still couldn't resist occasionally taking a listing with a larger contingency fee on the end in exchange for omitting the initial retainer (I've since learned better). At the closing table, the seller's attorney announced he thought the fee was too large and I could either take what he was offering or I could sue for all of it. The buyer, whom I did not represent but to whom I had sold two other businesses, immediately responded by saying he would not consummate a closing that did not honor all of the offer to purchase, a part of which called for my entire commission. He continued by saying if the seller could not afford it, he would pay it immediately and deduct it from the total price on the end of the note, which, with the proper paperwork, he did! No other buyer has ever come to my rescue and I don't expect their sympathy. Just like other professionals, I now get paid for what I do as I do it. More accurate and adequate paperwork attracts more fees. Protect your fees with the best agreements that can be lawfully prepared. It can be devastating to complete a project and then not get paid because your professional service agreement was not adequate.

BEWARE, BABY PORCUPINES CAN GROW INTO BIG ONES!

Most animals on our Texas farm that ended up being real beasts started out with cute little warm and fuzzy looks that made you want to be real cozy with them. The eventual time it takes to get secure in this business is like a baby porcupine; it doesn't look all that bad. Beware and be realistic about the initial investment of time, energy, and resources required. You don't plant an apple seed and expect to go out to the tree and pick apples the next day. Some of the best in the business required a significant start-up period. It's difficult to do your best work if one hand is hanging on to the financial panic button. Most who fail do so because they do not make adequate provisions for the inconsistency of what is largely a commission and/or fee structured career.

A part of the initial planning for entry into this type of career is the ability to understand the real value of money. Learn to spend less than you receive instead of trying to earn more than you can spend! With few exceptions, most of us get paid in money or some medium of exchange which we later trade for things we need. Most think the value of currency is measured in what it will purchase, and that's true, but it's not the entire truth. Another important part of the definition is the amount of personal time and energy consumed to earn it. We may all have different levels of performance, but we all have the same 24 hours per day in which to exercise these abilities for profit. You've just fooled yourself if you thought you came into this business so you would no longer have to work by the hour. The commissions and fees you earn must be divided by the hours it took to earn them. For example, if you purchased a $2 toothbrush, it did not just cost you $2. It really cost you a specific amount of time, of which you have a limited amount. Without this realization, you may fall into the most tempting trap of commission and/or fee structured careers which allures you into thinking you can now make all the money you can spend. When you commit to an expenditure, make sure what you are receiving is worth the hours you are spending wrestling with porcupines.

THE NEED FOR SURVIVAL

Another lesson we can learn from the animal kingdom is the need for survival. The porcupines I observed during my years on the farm spent most of their time maintaining a sufficient level of necessities for survival. Hopefully, those of us who are professionals will potentially earn a much greater level of achievement. Still, you must first learn to survive before you can succeed. Most of those I saw fail during the mid-80s did not fail because they could not sell. They failed because they could not survive between the sales. That economy did not allow any of us to make as many sales as fast as we were previously accustomed. Plan your budgets on a survival level, not on the extravagant level of your competitors. Downsizing is in style, enjoy it. Some professionals who once worked out of large expensive offices are now enjoying more success from the basements of their homes.

A professional's survival skills must include the ability to properly price his services according to his own abilities and performance. Why do some attorneys charge $50 per hour and others charge $5,000 per hour? It's because some are actually worth more than others and obviously perform at a level to justify the larger fees. *Fee cutters* end up being *service cutters* who ultimately ruin an industry for everyone, especially the clients! The provider of a service is entitled to the highest payment the market and their performance will support. Even if you have a perfect assignment, you are not reaching your best potential if you agree to work at the fee of the lowest bidder. So-called discounters seldom improve the quality of their product or service. Quality improvements in any product or service are made by those who can afford the cost of research and development (R&D). You will do a better job for your client and put more net dollars in your pocket by improving the quality of your services to warrant better fees instead of just negotiating lower fees to get business and then being forced to reduce the quality of service in the process.

Another necessity for survival is becoming aware of other opportunities for income within your industry. Don't let others provide services for your clients which can be professionally and adequately performed by you. If you are willing to be properly trained to do so, get involved in valuations, consulting, and other activities. If you are not adequately trained, team up and do the marketing for someone who is qualified. These are additional justified fees that help meet your cash flow requirements and make it possible to continue serving buyers and sellers while waiting for larger commissions and/or fees to be earned.

MORE PORCUPINE LESSONS

Back to the farm, I can also remember good lessons from more than porcupines. Fishing was a lot more productive than

hunting porcupines, with the result being in direct proportion to the quality of bait used. The same is true in selling
businesses. Better businesses attract better buyers. Avoid
nonsalable listings; they are nothing more than bad bait. You
not only waste time preparing the business for the market,
you waste more time and resources trying to sell it. Good
inventory is the most important aspect of this industry, and
it's the most important part of your business! If you don't
list a business for which there is some reasonable demand,
properly priced with a professional valuation, terms, and
return on investment, avoid it! Set minimum standards for
your listings, such as minimum net cash flow for manager/
owner salaries, adequate to attract better buyers. Make a list
of your personal minimum standards and adhere to these
goals. Speaking of standards, I now never list a business
unless a professional third-party valuation has been performed. I am firmly convinced that the intermediary should
not perform the valuation on his/her own listings. The number of professionals and buyers and sellers who agree with
me is growing fast as they learn no one wins in that process.
Tom West, editor of *The Business Broker,* says: "I believe all
businesses should have a third-party valuation. Unfortunately,
when the business broker performs the valuation, and subse-
quently tries to sell the business, he or she creates a trap that
many of them can't dig out of—how about that for a porcupine!"

Bigger is not always better (even though we thought so
when fishing in Texas). However, bigger businesses often
attract more qualified buyers with more money to spend. What
is the minimum average price for businesses on which you
will spend your time? It should be obvious that businesses
with larger prices also produce larger commissions. Trainers
in the insurance industry claim the income of insurance agents

is likely to mirror the income of the prospects on which they spend their time and energy. In the event this may be a universal reality for all salespersons, you should consider increasing your standards and avoid an overload of small projects.

Is there anything attractive about a porcupine? Well, if so, I never saw it and my personal contacts came accidentally, obviously not on purpose. Everything you see about the critters tells you to immediately leave them alone. Businesses can have the same look at times and need some real professional help in preparing them for the marketing process. Better *packaging* attracts more interested buyers. Use all of the marvelous techniques available in print, video, and electronics to make your product appealing. Fine tune your letters, telephone scripts, creative ads, and other communication media to meet the challenge of the twenty-first century. Improved cooperation and better sales are the result of improved communication skills and tools. Use them, don't be afraid of them, stay up-to-date.

WHAT'S WORSE THAN WRESTLING WITH A PORCUPINE?

If there is anything worse than wrestling with a porcupine, I suppose it would be wrestling with a whole bunch of them (how's that for Texas farm talking?). This is what happens when we allow small issues between buyers and sellers to grow into larger controversies which eventually involve legal professionals and courtrooms. Avoid conflicts and confrontations. These only add to your expense of doing business and never contribute more business. Be a problem solver and escape these wasted efforts. Failure, insecurity, and negative actions on the part of others cannot be allowed to become a part of your professional attitude and reputation.

The last courtroom I heard about an intermediary becoming involved in sounds like the largest gathering of porcupines to date. It's a long story, but the result was a lawsuit against the intermediary with both seller and buyer camps on the other side of the table and a $1,240,000 judgment against the intermediary firm. Now, do I have your attention?

The unfortunate part of the story is that this entire litigation process could have been avoided with *investigative due-diligence* from an independent third-party licensed private investigator before the principals signed the letter of intent! Background checks by a third-party licensed private investigator are a must on major players involved in buying and selling businesses.

Your first impression might be this is too small of a porcupine to worry about unless a large transaction is involved. Well, small porcupines can grow into large ones, and as we just discussed, they might grow into a large group of them. The minimum I recommend is that every intermediary at least suggest the idea to every seller and/or buyer they represent and make a note of the date and time of the suggestion. More can benefit from this suggestion than just the intermediary:

Sellers: Shouldn't sellers want to know if their company was being targeted by corporate raiders whose only motive was to steal what they had worked so hard to build?

Buyers: Do buyers really know enough about those with whom they are about to become involved? Buyers should want to know if the seller has skeletons in the closet.

Intermediaries: This service could help avoid future litigation for the professionals serving buyers and sellers. You would certainly want to know if a principal had a history of bankruptcy, tax liens, civil litigation, or especially a criminal record!

Bankers: In addition to background checks for reasons previously mentioned, bankers should seek assistance from CPAs, attorneys, and other professionals as well as licensed private investigators.

Attorneys: The important information secured in investigative due-diligence will not only prevent and/or assist in future litigation, but will improve the advice attorneys give their clients.

Accountants: In addition to avoiding future litigation, investigative due-diligence will assist in knowing who is being dealt with, having access to their true history and financial situations, and providing more current and accurate information in reports.

In addition to personal and corporate background checks on potential players in transactions, there are numerous other services provided by reputable licensed private investigators and/or legal professionals. Check the following list for appropriate services on each transaction in which you are involved, or you may find porcupine quills creeping into your neat little nest:

Corporate Services:
   Registered agent
   Incorporation/qualification
   Limited liability companies
   Name reservation/registration
   Limited partnerships

Corporate kits

Tax clearance

Good standing certificate

Shelf corporation

Name saver corporation

Corporate and LP status reports

Corporate status/verification searches

Franchise tax searches

Assumed name and D/B/A searches

Corporate staffing

Forms/precedents/outlines

Tax notices

Corporate document retrieval

Federal tax ID number

Corporate officer and director research

Corporate document filing/preparation

Name clearance/availability

Delaware holding company

Trademark searches (state and federal)

Patent searches

Secured transaction services:

UCC filing/preparation (1,2,3 state and local)

UCC searches (state/local)

UCC reflective searches

UCC forms

UCC filing control system

Federal and state tax liens

Purchase money security and letters of notification

Instant access to microfilm libraries

Mechanic's lien searches

Real property searches

Grantor/grantee index

Secured party searches

Suits and judgements searches

Motor vehicle searches

Court record research:

Federal, state, and local courts

Research and retrieval

U.S. bankruptcy court

Appellate court research/retrieval

Supreme court research/retrieval

Index summary

International:

Offshore incorporations

Legalization/authentication

International registered agent services

Since it is the responsibility of the client to pay for these services, there are no negative reasons for a professional to not recommend them, and every positive reason exists for them to do so. It is not necessary to burden the transaction of a small retail business with the paperwork required to purchase General Motors. However, taking shortcuts in the minimum logical steps just to save time and expenses is nothing but a potential porcupine ride to the courthouse for all involved!

PESTICIDES FOR PORCUPINES!

The porcupine story could go on forever and the best part is that porcupines can be avoided. Every time I attend a major convention of intermediaries I hear more war stories that should be added to the list. Professionals involved in the buying, selling, and valuing of businesses should participate in a minimum of two continuing educational opportunities each year. As you learn from others, you should make your own list of porcupines and be consistent in your commitment to avoid them. I sincerely hope most of your career stories will be warm and fuzzy ones, totally void of any porcupine quills!

4

FINDING BUYERS AND SELLERS OF BUSINESSES

Sellers want to sell and need help in finding the appropriate buyers. Buyers want to buy and need help in finding the right businesses. Both sellers and buyers seldom know how to coordinate all of the complicated activity to a satisfactory conclusion. Because they cannot easily locate each other and conduct proper confidential negotiations there is a transaction vacuum, relatively void of any action until the properly trained professional gets them together to initiate and coordinate the process. This professional is often called the intermediary, business broker, business sales consultant, M&A specialist, business counselor, or one of other titles.

The main task of this professional in business sales is often to go where there is no immediate action, locate all parties needed in a transaction, and generate enthusiastic participation that consummates in a closing. In common sales terms, this professional must not only find a properly motivated and capable buyer, he/she must also create or at least locate the product. Consequently, when most enter this profession, not only do they not have any buyers, they don't even have anything to sell.

SOONER OR LATER, EVERYONE NEEDS AN INTERMEDIARY!

So where does an intermediary (or whichever title you choose to use) start, with a seller or a buyer? After more than 25 years of searching for sellers and buyers, I am firmly convinced they are both found through the same processes and most will become interchangeable. The theory that you first look for sellers and then start the search for the perfect match in a buyer may be an antiquated, clumsy, and inefficient use of time and resources. A more logical and profitable exercise could be to give everyone an opportunity to become a seller, buyer, purchase a valuation, or all three! I jokingly tell everyone I'm like an undertaker, sooner or later they will need me. If they do not have either of these needs currently, I give them a chance to refer to me others within their circle of influence who need any of my services.

This exercise allows a minimum of four opportunities of success for the intermediary. Every communication could potentially produce a seller, buyer, valuation, referral, possibly all four or more. If you are not aware of the current need(s) of the person with whom you are about to communicate, which opportunity do you give them first? It doesn't matter, just be sure to give them all four chances to make your day!

THIS IS A SERIOUS RESPONSIBILITY

The fact a seller has given a specific intermediary a sole and exclusive right to sell for a year (52 weeks) or a buyer has given an exclusive right to search for a business are very significant factors. It is a serious element of trust on the part of buyers and sellers and a marvelous opportunity for intermediaries.

Sellers agree to spend all efforts in continuing to grow the business and expect the intermediary to use every known process to find the right buyer. Buyers work hard to assemble proper financial resources to consummate a transaction. To properly represent these principals (usually one at a time) an intermediary must consider more steps in the process than simply running an ad in the newspaper and waiting for the telephone to ring!

RESOURCES ARE ABUNDANT . . .
OVER 52 AVAILABLE!

There are many successful steps used to find buyers and sellers of businesses. After consulting with seasoned intermediaries, I compiled a list which has been proven by some of the finest in the industry. There are 52 included in this chapter because it provides a different intermediary buyer/seller/referral activity for each week in a year. Several intermediaries who have adopted these steps have capitalized on the idea of marketing their services by promising to do something different each week of the year instead of repeating the same steps over and over. This is often very impressive to buyers and sellers, especially if they are considering using the services of an intermediary who cannot even name 10 different steps.

One of the most important characteristics of successful professionals is their commitment to make specific plans which they monitor regularly with an accurate record system. Goals are worthless unless the professional uses discipline to follow them and make honest evaluations of the results. The 52 Steps Checklist is provided in Exhibit 4.1 to assist in accomplishing this proven principle. Since the steps presented in this chapter are not necessarily in the correct order for any given assignment, write in the name of the step which corresponds to the week in which you plan to initiate the step and then monitor your progress.

Each of the 52 steps provides a completely different activity which will result in new prospects provided by the source. A brief explanation precedes the specific steps, sources, and/or persons to contact for potential buyers and sellers. You may choose some of the specific sources from a list at the end of this chapter to jump start your process. Even though many of the motivations for these persons helping you may be the same, some will respond better if you will make a list of unique ways to more appropriately stimulate each group.

INDEX OF 52 STEPS TO FIND BUYERS AND SELLERS OF BUSINESSES

Primary resources

Step 1: Advertising
Step 2: Marketing within your own office
Step 3: Your personal circle of influence
Step 4: Co-op with other intermediary offices

Professional resources

Step 5: Accountants and attorneys
Step 6: Real estate agents and A.C.G. (Association for Corporate Growth)

Exhibit 4.1

52 Steps Checklist

Seller/Buyer:_____Start Date:_/_/_End Date:_/_/_

Week	Step	Completed	Week	Step	Completed
1	_____	_/_/_	2	_____	_/_/_
3	_____	_/_/_	4	_____	_/_/_
5	_____	_/_/_	6	_____	_/_/_
7	_____	_/_/_	8	_____	_/_/_
9	_____	_/_/_	10	_____	_/_/_
11	_____	_/_/_	12	_____	_/_/_
13	_____	_/_/_	14	_____	_/_/_
15	_____	_/_/_	16	_____	_/_/_
17	_____	_/_/_	18	_____	_/_/_
19	_____	_/_/_	20	_____	_/_/_
21	_____	_/_/_	22	_____	_/_/_
23	_____	_/_/_	24	_____	_/_/_
25	_____	_/_/_	26	_____	_/_/_
27	_____	_/_/_	28	_____	_/_/_
29	_____	_/_/_	30	_____	_/_/_
31	_____	_/_/_	32	_____	_/_/_
33	_____	_/_/_	34	_____	_/_/_
35	_____	_/_/_	36	_____	_/_/_
37	_____	_/_/_	38	_____	_/_/_
39	_____	_/_/_	40	_____	_/_/_
41	_____	_/_/_	42	_____	_/_/_
43	_____	_/_/_	44	_____	_/_/_
45	_____	_/_/_	46	_____	_/_/_
47	_____	_/_/_	48	_____	_/_/_
49	_____	_/_/_	50	_____	_/_/_
51	_____	_/_/_	52	_____	_/_/_

Additional Steps Used By Intermediary

__	_____	_/_/_	__	_____	_/_/_
__	_____	_/_/_	__	_____	_/_/_
__	_____	_/_/_	__	_____	_/_/_
__	_____	_/_/_	__	_____	_/_/_
__	_____	_/_/_	__	_____	_/_/_

Step 7: Insurance agents
Step 8: Appraisers
Step 9: Engineers
Step 10: Politicians
Step 11: Networking groups, clubs, and civic organizations

Resources within the industry

Step 12: Industry/trade lists
Step 13: Competitors
Step 14: Substitute products and services
Step 15: Related products
Step 16: Direct customers
Step 17: Related customers
Step 18: Direct suppliers and providers
Step 19: Related suppliers and providers
Step 20: Distributors
Step 21: Diversification
Step 22: Consultant, management, and representatives

Resources in the financial community

Step 23: Commercial bankers
Step 24: Other commercial banking providers
Step 25: Investment bankers
Step 26: Investment advisors
Step 27: SBA and other specialty loan packages
Step 28: Loan brokers
Step 29: High net worth individuals
Step 30: Movers and shakers

Resources within the same geographical area

Step 31: Landlords
Step 32: Other business owners in the same area
Step 33: Windshield survey
Step 34: Door-to-door "hot calls"

Resources from qualified civic and other "people sources"

Step 35: Municipal
Step 36: Educational
Step 37: Retirement groups
Step 38: Employment outplacement centers and executive recruiters
Step 39: Immigration attorneys

Resources within the circle of influence of the principals for whom you are working

Step 40: Ask the buyer or seller for prospects

Resources found in restructure possibilities

Step 41: ESOPs
Step 42: Investment groups
Step 43: Partnerships
Step 44: Restructure within current ownership
Step 45: Syndications
Step 46: Mergers
Step 47: 1031 tax-deferred exchange

Step 48: Trade possibilities

Step 49: Conglomerates

Step 50: Asset auction

Step 51: Other uses of the assets

Step 52: Bankruptcy

Step 1   Advertising

The main purpose of this section is to make available many successful marketing ideas in addition to advertising. However, advertising is still a very important step and may be one of the first you will need to consider. In preparing your print ads it is important to be brief, but not to the point you become confusing. Use of the grid in Exhibit 4.2 may be helpful in designing ads. Notice the first line of each grid is shorter than the other five, because capital and/or bold letters are normally used for the first word(s) which require more space. A good exercise is to design five different ads and then choose the one most appropriate.

Use the following to determine where you will place your ads:

1. Local newspapers

2. Regional newspapers

3. National/international newspapers

4. Local trade publications

5. Regional trade publications

6. National/international trade publications

7. Check for buyers and sellers who advertise in each of the above

8. The Internet

    (a) Industry business transfer databases

    (b) Your own page

Exhibit 4.2

Grid for Use in Designing Newspaper Ads

Note: The first line of each grid has three fewer spaces because the first word in each ad is normally printed in bold and/or capital letters which require more space per letter.

At this writing there are potentially 40 million users who can be reached by your use of the Internet. Our company currently has listings in three business transfer databases as well as our own home page. I was recently contacted by a buyer in Waco, Texas who found me through one of the industry databases. Within six weeks of the initial contact, he became the happy owner of one of my listings in Colorado. The fees earned from this one sale could cover my Internet costs for many years. Several of the industry database providers are listed in the Industry Resource Section at the back of this book. Some of them will also develop and manage your own home page.

9. Add your own advertising ideas

Step 2   Marketing Within Your Own Office

The best place to test your marketing materials is with the other professionals in your office. They may have just the perfect match for your buyer or seller needs. Consider the following possible ideas for your own office before you reach for the universe:

1. Place a finished copy of your marketing package or search criteria on the desk of every professional in your office as soon as it is in the finished form.

2. Arrange to make a presentation to the next regular meeting of the professionals in your office. Bring your buyer or seller to this staff meeting and use a specific, timed outline, and include your buyer or seller in your presentation. Tell your buyer or seller this is a rehearsal for the first meeting you will have with the potential match you

will eventually find for them. Develop the following suggested outline for the meeting in your office:

Intermediary introduce all parties involved

Seller or buyer give brief history of business for sale or criteria for business wanted

Visual presentation(s)

Present specific financial aspects

Questions and answers

3. Following this group presentation, speak individually to each professional in the meeting and ask them to make suggestions for improvements to your presentation.

4. Make periodic inquiries of them to keep your needs fresh in their minds.

5. When you make changes in your project, be sure to give them updated materials.

6. Other ideas.

Step 3   Your Personal Circle of Influence

Over a period of time you will develop a circle of influence, including a growing number of individuals with whom you have had previous communications regarding valuing, buying, and selling businesses. Since your name and the services you provide are familiar to these people, they should be among the first you contact regarding this new opportunity. Consider the following possibilities for the development and continued growth of your circle of influence:

1. Those you know who have bought and/or sold:

Businesses in the same or similar SIC codes

Businesses in the same price range

Businesses in the same general geographical area

2. Those you know who have been and are still prospects for the above.

3. The new persons with whom you talk on a daily basis about other opportunities should be considered possible *switches* to this opportunity.

4. Ask for referrals as you confidentially share this opportunity on a daily basis. If you are not already doing so, purchase one of the excellent computer programs which allow you to easily keep and access records of the above activities.

5. Others.

Step 4   Co-op With Other Intermediary Offices

The buyer or seller has engaged the intermediary to use his/ her best efforts to sell or locate a business. Even though the intermediary will need to share some fees and/or commissions, a co-op may be in the best interest of the buyer or seller. Proper agency agreements required by the state(s) in which you operate and confidentiality statements must accompany these activities. Another type of cooperation often used among professionals is done on a referral basis. One intermediary firm takes complete control of the transaction and simply pays a referral fee to the firm which provides the other side of the deal. This offers better control and often results in a more confidential process. It is important that all parties involved in sharing fees and commissions be properly licensed to do so. Consider some of these possibilities:

1. Local intermediary offices
2. Intermediary offices in your state
3. Intermediary offices across the nation
4. International intermediary offices
5. National/international network organizations
6. Franchise groups of intermediaries
7. Others

Step 5   Accountants and Attorneys

These professionals have business contacts which are capable of participating in transactions of all types and financial requirements. You will want to contact them on a local, state, and national basis.

1. Accountants
2. Attorneys

Step 6   Real Estate Agents and ACG

Many people who move from one area to another also buy and sell businesses when they move. It is important to keep good relationships within this industry.

1. Real estate agents
2. Real estate brokers
3. Real estate developers
4. Private and institutional real estate schools

5. The Association for Corporate Growth (ACG) is a professional organization with active chapters all across the United States which includes real estate professionals as well as influential persons from many other industries.

   (a) Local

   (b) State

   (c) National

Step 7   **Insurance Agents**

The insurance industry touches every segment of the population, especially those with financial resources to buy and sell businesses. They are found in at least three categories:

1. Health and life agents
2. Property and casualty agents
3. Multi-line agents (both of the above)

Step 8   **Appraisers**

It is normally considered a conflict of interest for appraisers to represent buyers and sellers when they are providing appraisals for the businesses involved. This makes them a wonderful source of referrals. You will find them in several categories:

1. Business appraisers
2. Equipment appraisers
3. Real estate appraisers
4. Others

Step 9   Engineers

Engineers are found serving almost every industry. It is in their interest to know who may have a need for buying and/ or selling businesses. Obviously, they want to keep good relations with business owners to keep their cash flow secure. They will help you find the missing part(s) of your potential transaction.

Step 10   Politicians

These individuals know a lot of people. Since they are prone to want to ask favors, why not ask a few of them?

1. Local
2. State
3. National
4. Others

Step 11   Clubs, Organizations, and Networking Groups

I once purchased lists of these groups in the city in which I was working and found hundreds which could be helpful in finding buyers and sellers. You will want to become a member of only a few of them but will find leaders in others who will help you.

One of the most successful business brokers in Texas offers his services as a speaker for these groups from which he receives almost all of his potential buyers and sellers (and a lot of free meals).

1. Ones in which you hold membership
2. Ones in which you have *contacts*
3. Ones in which you are offering to be a speaker
4. Others

Step 12   Industry Trade Lists

There are many sources of lists within each individual trade which will provide names to be turned into potential buyers and sellers. Below are just a few which should be the basic ones to try in each industry.

1. General business guides printed for sale in your local metro area
2. Industrial directories provided by:
   (a) Local government agencies
   (b) State government agencies
   (c) State educational agencies
3. Dunn's and other proprietary services
   (a) Primary SIC codes of the business with which you are working
   (b) Total SIC codes including primary and secondary products
   (c) Executives in the industry
4. Trade associations lists
   (a) Local
   (b) Regional
   (c) State
   (d) National

(e)   Periodicals published in the industry
5.   Others

Step 13   Competitors

Confidentiality is always a concern and especially when communicating with specific competitors. However, some of the best prospects are among those found in these lists. Be sure to clear these actions with your seller and/or buyer before proceeding.

1.   Yellow pages
     (a)   Local/regional
     (b)   State/national
2.   Secure lists from your buyer and/or seller
3.   Ask trade show promoters for their lists
     (a)   Local trade show promoters
     (b)   Local trade show suppliers, decorators, and so on
     (c)   Regional/national of above
     (d)   Franchise/business opportunity promoters of all
4.   Names from individual trade lists

Step 14   Substitute Products and Services

Many products and services experience competition from others who offer substitutes. Herein lies a whole new group of buyers and sellers who should be offered the opportunity to invest or divest with you. Use all of your list resources.

1. Local/regional
2. State/national

Step 15 Related Products

Most products and services are used in connection with other products within their industry. This synergy provides you additional lists of buyers and sellers. Use all your list resources.

1. Local
2. Regional
3. State
4. National

Step 16 Direct Customers

Confidentiality is a real concern, but do not allow it to cause you to avoid this wonderful source of buyers and sellers. In addition to your normal resources of lists, ask the buyer or seller with whom you are working for their assistance and approval.

1. Current customers of buyer or seller with whom you are working.
2. Develop a list of others who should be customers within the trade area.
3. Consider potential customers outside of the current trade area:

(a) Regional
(b) State
(c) National
(d) International

Step 17   Related Customers

Customers of related products and services provide you with another source of buyers and sellers. Use all of your list resources.

1. Local
2. Regional
3. State
4. National
5. International
6. Others

Step 18   Direct Suppliers and Providers

Suppliers in the industry make it their business to know who is interested in making changes, both investing and divesting. Make sure you give them the opportunity to assist you. Their motivation is that you will encourage the buyer or seller to do business with them.

1. Suppliers of products and merchandise
2. Providers of services
3. Providers of personnel
4. Others

Step 19　Related Suppliers and Providers

Here again, the synergy of those within the industry who are secondary suppliers and providers of other products and services gives you more prospective buyers and sellers:

1. Local
2. Regional
3. State
4. National
5. International
6. Others

Step 20　Distributors

Wholesale distributors in the industry are excellent sources of buyers and sellers. They are definitely interested in maintaining their current customers and creating new ones and will be helpful to you in both categories.

1. Current products
2. Current services
3. Related products
4. Related services
5. Products and services that could be used for expansion of the business
6. Others

Step 21   Diversification

Consider the potential names of buyers and sellers available through diversification within and outside the industry.

1. Other products within the industry
2. Other services within the industry
3. New products within the industry
4. New services within the industry
5. Other industries

Step 22   Consultant, Management Companies, and Representatives

People who provide consultant and management services and manufacturers' representatives within the industry are great sources of names of buyers and sellers. It is their job to know the potential movers and shakers.

1. Consultants
2. Management companies
3. Sales representatives in the industry
4. Others

Step 23   Commercial Bankers

In addition to helping you locate those capable of becoming qualified buyers, commercial bankers will occasionally assist owners in divesting of their businesses for a variety of reasons, hopefully good ones. You should keep this network active on a regular basis.

1. Commercial bankers within the immediate geographical area
2. Commercial bankers within the metro area
3. Commercial bankers within the region
4. Commercial bankers within the state
5. National and international commercial bankers
6. Others

Step 24   Other Commercial Banking Providers

Providers of specialty services in the commercial financial community, such as merchant bankers, equipment leasing companies, factoring companies, and others are in constant contact with potential buyers and sellers. Keep your lines of communication open with them, especially with definite needs on which you are currently working.

1. Merchant bankers (depositories of bank card transactions)
2. Bank card marketing companies
3. Equipment leasing companies
4. Factoring companies (short-term financing of accounts receivable, etc.)
5. Others

Step 25   Investment Bankers

Investment bankers assist companies in raising capital, issue corporate securities, market corporate securities, and other services (Europeans used to call them merchant bankers). They will often have buyers and sellers in their acquaintance which do not fit into their normal activities and will be glad to refer them to you. Keep good relationships with them and work on a financial referral basis with them.

1. Local

2. Regional

3. State

4. National

5. International

6. Others

Step 26   Investment Advisors

These licensed professionals sell financial products to people who have money to invest. You need to get to know them because they know the people with investment capabilities.

1. Investment advisors

2. Certified financial planners

3. Stockbrokers

4. Others

Step 27 SBA and Other Specialty Loan Packagers

These specialty packagers network with a lot of buyers and sellers and can become a great source of prospects for you.

1. SBA packagers
2. Other federally guaranteed loan packagers
3. City, community, county, and other local loan packagers
4. State funded and/or guaranteed loan packagers
5. Others

Step 28 Loan Brokers

Loan brokers work in every area of finance and can be helpful to you in finding buyers and sellers of businesses.

1. SBA and other federally guaranteed loans
2. City, community, county, and other locally funded and/or guaranteed loans
3. State funded and/or guaranteed loans
4. Equipment loans
5. Commercial loans
6. Bond brokers
7. Others

Step 29	**High Net Worth Individuals**

(People with money who wish not to be visible)

Over a period of time you should compile a list of high net worth individuals from a variety of sources. Every time you have a need for a buyer or seller you should check this list for the right person, or at least a referral. I have found these names on membership lists of exclusive clubs, charity donations, and so on.

1. Exclusive clubs
2. Charity donations lists
3. Others

Step 30	**Movers and Shakers**

(People with money who like to be visible)

Each time you read a newspaper or other periodical, collect the names of persons who have made the financial news because of their financial moves. Keep these in appropriate files for use when you have a need for a buyer or seller.

1. Local newspaper(s)
2. Local business news publications
3. National newspaper(s)
4. Radio news
5. Television
6. Internet
7. Others

Step 31   Landlords

Landlords are occasionally potential buyers of businesses and almost always can provide good prospects for buyers and sellers. With the approval of the business owner, contact the following:

1. Landlord of the business in question
2. Landlords of similar businesses in the area
3. Landlords of other businesses in the area
4. Landlords of similar businesses in other areas
5. Others

Step 32   Other Business Owners in the Same Area

If business owners believe in the financial strength of the area in which they own a business, they may consider owning another in the same area. Give them a call.

1. Owners of the same type of business in the area
2. Owners of different types of businesses in the area
3. General business investors in the area
4. Others

Step 33   Windshield Survey

You should immediately purchase a small handheld recorder to carry in your vehicle at all times. As you move about the city, look out your windshield at every business and make a note on the recorder of those which appear to fit into the requirements of the businesses with which you are willing to work. When you return to the office, look up the owners and call to make buyers and sellers out of them. The names who then qualify for your time will be:

1. Used in current needs
2. Potential searches and/or listings
3. Placed in proper files for future use
4. Others

Step 34   Door to Door *Hot Calls*

I choose to call this canvassing *hot calls* rather than cold calling because we are the ones who should determine the *temperature* of these person-to-person communications. In smaller businesses, this may be an effective prospecting source for buyers and sellers.

1. Shopping centers
2. Strip malls
3. Industrial parks

Step 35   Municipal

There are several municipal resources of buyers and sellers in every major metropolitan area. Their equivalents are available in smaller areas. One of their services is to assist buyers, investors, and others in locating business opportunities in their city and state. Make friends with them and call regularly to remind them you are here to help them do their job.

1. Chambers of commerce
2. Economic development council(s)
3. The mayor's office
4. The governor's office
5. Others

Step 36 Educational

Most of the educational institutions in your area can provide names of potential buyers and sellers.

1. Some of the graduates of trade schools come from families who are financially qualified to assist them in becoming owners of businesses instead of just employees.
2. Colleges and universities often have inquiries from buyers and sellers.
3. Professional continuing educational schools have good potential buyers and sellers come through their doors.
4. Others

Step 37 Retirement Groups

Retirement organizations have members who still have ambitions and money to qualify as buyers and sellers.

1. AARP
2. SCORE
3. Industry-sponsored groups
4. Others

Step 38 — Employment Outplacement Centers and Executive Recruiters

Many employers provide assistance to former employees in their search for new income opportunities. These are often good places to find prospects for smaller businesses. Executive recruiters are willing to work with you at times.

1. Centers sponsored by local employers
2. Independently owned centers in your area
3. Centers sponsored by government agencies
4. Executive recruiters (check Yellow Pages and classified ads, etc.)
5. Others

Step 39 — Immigration Attorneys

Federal legislation has provided opportunities to locate buyers and sellers who will be making residency changes through the purchase of businesses.

1. Local immigration attorneys
2. Regional immigration attorneys
3. National immigration attorneys
4. Others

Step 40 — Ask the Buyer or Seller for Names

When you are working with a seller, and adequate time has passed to allow you to develop confidence, ask for prospects. The same is applicable when you are doing a buyer search.

1. Family members who might be interested
2. Professional contacts of your buyers and sellers
3. Friends, competitors, or anyone who might become interested
4. Individual employees
5. Others

Step 41 ESOPs

An employee stock option plan could become the perfect buyer for a business and some of them may become sellers for you. Unless you have special training in this area, I suggest you secure the professional services of those who have this expertise. Check with the local bar association and CPA organizations.

1. ESOP attorneys
2. ESOP accountants
3. ESOP packagers
4. ESOP loan brokers
5. Others

Step 42 Investment Groups

Many investment groups specialize in buying and selling businesses. These are everywhere and come in a variety of types.

1. Professional investment group managers
2. Local investment clubs

3. Investment corporations

4. Others

Step 43　Partnerships

This is another legal form of ownership used by many to buy and sell businesses. Over a period of time you should develop a large list of them.

1. General partnerships

2. Family partnerships

3. Limited partnerships

4. Others

Step 44　Restructure Within Current Ownership

1. One or more of the partners buy out the other(s)

2. Partial sale

3. Incorporation and so on

Step 45　Syndications

If you are properly certified to do so, you may create syndications to purchase businesses. Some existing syndications become excellent sellers.

1. Existing syndications

2. Create new syndications

Step 46   Mergers

The subject of mergers is worth a full volume within itself. Merger potentials with other businesses create many opportunities for transactions.

1. Merger for expansion

2. Merger for financial assistance

3. Merger to access additional:

   (a) Products

   (b) Services

   (c) Clients

   (d) Employees

   (e) Territories

   (f) Patents

   (g) Others

Step 47   1031 Tax-deferred Exchange

Special tax advantages encourage this as a vehicle for buyers and sellers in some special instances. If you do not have adequate training and experience in these exchanges, seek professional assistance.

1. Sellers

2. Buyers

Step 48   Trade Possibilities

Trades that do not qualify for 1031 tax-deferred exchanges can also be accomplished when a buyer or seller is willing to accept only part of their desired needs.

1. Trade in on a business of another type
2. Trade up for a larger business of the same type
3. Trade down for a business of a smaller size
4. Others

Step 49   Conglomerates

Conglomerates are usually made up of different companies in different industries. Secure the identities of these who can become both buyers and sellers in and out of the industries in which they currently operate.

1. Within the industry in which you are working
2. Other industries
3. Others

Step 50   Asset Auction

This is not necessarily an exciting option to a seller, but may be a wonderful opportunity for a buyer. Be sure that you are properly licensed or seek the assistance of someone who is experienced.

1. Real property
2. Personal property

Step 51   Other Uses of the Assets

If all else fails, consider a higher and better use of the assets. Maybe the property needs to be used for a completely different type of business.

Step 52   Bankruptcy

Bankruptcy provides solutions for both sellers and buyers. It is necessary that your agreement with principals is adequately confirmed by the bankruptcy court.

Use Your Imagination!

Since my goal was to present 52 different steps for 52 weeks in the year, I had to omit many. Use your imagination and continue the process.

EXAMPLES OF RESOURCE LISTS TO ASSIST YOU IN FINDING BUYERS AND SELLERS OF BUSINESSES

Time and space do not allow, nor is it necessary, to print a complete list of all resources available of names, addresses, and telephone numbers of leads to find buyers and sellers of businesses. This list will *jump-start* your process and hopefully motivate you to constantly add to your own personal list. Almost every resource on this list can be found in your local business library at no cost to you. Many are also available on the Internet and CD-ROM.

AARP
3200 E. Carson St.
Lakewood, CA 90712

Accountants Directory
See *Thomas Publishing Co.* or
    Dun and Bradstreet

American Bar Association
750 N. Lake Shore Dr.
Chicago, IL 60611

American Business Lists
P. O. Box 27347
Omaha, NE 68127
402-593-4600
E-mail: directory@abii.com

America's Phone Book
150,000 Corporations,
    Government Agencies and
    Toll Free Numbers
Simon & Schuster
Distributed by Prentice Hall
800-722-3244
Lists of over 10 Million
    Businesses (available by
    state)

Appraisal Institute
Boulevard Tower-N. Ste. 724
225 N. Michigan Ave.
Chicago, IL 60601-7601

*Association of Machine and
    Equipment Appraisers*
1110 Spring St.
Silver Springs, MD 20910
301-587-9335

*Brand Names: Who Owns
    What*
Facts on File Publishers
New York, NY

Brands and Their Companies
(3 volumes)
Gale Research
See *American Business Lists*

Business Brokers Directory
See *American Business Lists*

*Business Capital Sources IWS
    Inc.*
24 Canterbury Rd.
Rockville Centre, NY 11570
516-766-5850

*Cumulative List of
    Organizations*
Department of the Treasury,
    IRS
U.S. Government Printing
    Office
Washington, DC 20402

Directories in Print (2 volumes)
Charles B. Montney, Editor
Gale Research, Inc.
835 Penobscot Bldg.
Detroit, MI 48226-4094

Directory of Engineers in Practice
National Society of
  Professional Engineers
1420 King St.
Alexandria, VA 22314

Directory of Foreign Manufacturers in the U.S.
Georgia State University
  Business Press
College of Business
  Administration
Atlanta, GA

Directory of M&A Intermediaries
Venture Economics, Inc.
617-449-2100

Directory of Mfg.
Available in many states.
Published by Varmes Pub. Co.

Directory of Small Business Investment Companies
Small Business Association
1441 L St. N.W. Room 808
Washington, DC 20416
202-653-6672

Directory of Texas Manufacturers (also available in some other states)
Bureau of Business Research
U of T @ Austin
P.O. Box 7459
Austin, TX 78713-7459
512-471-1616

Directory of Texas Wholesalers (also available in some other states)
See *Directory of Texas Manufacturers*

Dun and Bradstreet Catalog of Business Mailing Lists and Direct Marketing Services
3 Sylvan Way
Parsippany, NJ 07054-9978
800-624-5669

Dun's Directory of Service Companies

Dun's Industrial Guide

Emerson's Directory of Leading U.S. Accounting Firms
Redmond, VA

Encyclopedia of Associations (3 volumes)
Deborah M. Burek, Editor

ESOP Association
1100 17th St. N.W. Ste. 1207
Washington, DC 20036
202-293-2971

FIABCI-USA
(International R.E. Federation)

Financial Planners and
Planning Organizations
Directories
Omnigraphics, Inc.
Penobscot Bldg.
645 Griswold, 24th Floor
Detroit, MI 48226
313-961-1340

Financial Planning
Consultants Directory
American Business Directory,
Inc.
See *Thomas Register*

Forbes Directory of
Organizations
713-524-0409

Franchise Opportunities
Handbook
U. S. Department of
Commerce
U. S. Government Printing
Office
Washington, DC 20402

Investment Management
Consultants Association
10200 E. Girard, Ste. 3400
Denver, CO 80231
303-337-2424

IREM
(Institute of R. E.
Management)

League of Women Voters
713-552-1776

Leasing Companies Directory
American Business Directory
See *Thomas Register*

Leasing Sourcebook:
The Directory of the U. S.
Capital Leasing Industry
Bibliotechnology System and
Publishing Company
P.O. Box 657
Lincoln, MA 01773
617-259-0524

Loan Broker Annual Directory
Loan Broker
P. O. Box 1553
Owosso, MI 48867

Loans Directory
American Business Directory
See *Thomas Register*

Local Associations of CPAs

Local Association of Health/
Life Underwriters

Local Association of Property/
Casualty Ins. Agents

Local Associations of
Property Exchange

Local Associations of Realtors

Local Bar Association(s)

Local Business Publications

Local Chamber of Commerce

Local Economic Development
Council

Local Financial Planners
Association

Local Machine and
Equipment Appraisers

Local Society of Engineers

Local White Pages

Local Yellow Pages

Macmillian Directory of
Leading Private
Companies
National Register Publishing
Co.
3004 Glenview Rd.
Wilmette, IL 60091
708-441-2210

Manufacturer's News, Inc.
(90+/- different books of
business lists by county
and state)
1633 Central St.
Evanston, IL 60201-1505
708-864-7000

Martindale-Hubble Law
Directory
(19 volumes)

Moody's International Manual
of Investment Companies
Moody's Investors Service,
Inc.
Dun and Bradstreet
Corporation
99 Church St.
New York, NY 10007
212-553-0300

Nation-List International
800-525-9559

National Association of CPAs

National Association of
Health/Life Underwriters

National Association of
Property/Casualty Ins.
Agents

National Association of
Realtors
312-329-8200

National Financial Planners
Association

National Million Dollar
Directory and Leading
Public and Private
Companies
Dun and Bradstreet

National Property Exchange
Organization

Political Action Groups

Polk Bank Directory
(International Edition)
See next

Polk Bank Directory (National
American Edition)
R. L. Polk and Company,
Publishing
2001 Elm Hill Pike
Nashville, TN 37210-3848
800-827-2265

*Realtors National Marketing
    Institute*
312-321-4411

*SBIC Directory and
    Handbook of Small
    Business Financing*
International Wealth Success,
    Inc.
24 Canterbury Rd.
Rockville Centre, NY 11570
516-766-5850

SCORE
1825 Connecticut Ave. N.W.
    Ste. 503
Washington, DC 20009

*SIC (Standard Industrial
    Code) Manual*
Order No. PB 87-100012
National Technical
    Information Service
5285 Port Royal Rd.
Springfield, VA 22161
202-653-6279

SIOR
(Society of Industrial and
    Office Realtors)

State Associations of CPAs

*State Association of Health/
    Life Underwriters*

*State Association of Property/
    Casualty Ins. Agents*

*State Associations of Property
    Exchange*

State Associations of Realtors

State Bar Association(s)

*State Business Guide
    Directories*

State Chamber of Commerce

State Directory of Politicians

*State Economic Development
    Council*

*State Financial Planners
    Association*

State Legal Directories

*State Machine and Equipment
    Appraisers*

State Society of Engineers

*Telephone Directories in
    Other Cities*
Call: 800-SWB-BOOK

Texas Banking Red Book (also
    available in most other
    states)
Texas Bankers Association
203 W. Tenth
Austin, TX 78701
512-472-8388

Thomas Publishing Co.
One Penn Plaza
New York, NY 10117-0138

*Thomas Register of American
    Mfg.*
See address above

*Thomas Register of Company
    Profiles*
See address above

*Thomas Register of Products
    and Services* (many
    volumes)

*U.S. Directory of Registered
    Investment Advisory with
    the SEC*
Money Market Directory, Inc.
Box 1608
Charlottesville, VA 22902
804-977-1450

Venture Capital Directory
Forum Publishing Company
383 E. Main
Centerport, NY 11721
516-754-5000

Women's Council of Realtors

World M&A Network
202-628-6900

5

INITIAL CONTACT WITH PROSPECTIVE SELLERS AND BUYERS

Icebreakers can be deal breakers if not properly handled by the professional who is looking for the principal(s) necessary to create a transaction. Since we only have one opportunity to create a favorable first impression, it is worthwhile to spend time and resources in the development of effective communication tools. These initial contacts are for the purpose of making appointments, not making deals. Don't confuse the two. You make deals after you meet face-to-face.

Professionals involved in the sales of businesses should never fool themselves into thinking there is an easier way to sell anything, especially big-ticket items, than person-to-person communication skills! Consequently, take advantage of every opportunity to improve these necessary skills to control your own destiny. Regardless of the current state of the economy or the lack of effectiveness of the latest advertisement efforts, you can put yourself in a profitable position when you pick up the phone and personally start the process to create a transaction.

DEVELOPING PERSON-TO-PERSON COMMUNICATION SKILLS

This book is not a collection of new gimmicks to keep professionals from having to locate and deal with principals of transactions. It is a selection of proven ideas to increase your skills in dealing directly with users of your valuation and intermediary services. Sooner or later you must use your personal skills just as the surgeon does his own surgery and the quarterback takes the ball in his own hands.

Advertising, seminars, mailings, brochures, calling cards, networking, the Internet, and other effective marketing tools are helpful and almost all successful professionals use them. However, you ultimately will have to deal directly with the people who will be involved to get the job done. Why not sooner than later?

Too many in our profession mail letters, place ads in a variety of places, and then sit in a chair with their feet on the desk and wait for the phone to ring. They place too much of their success in the hands of others.

The professionals I know who are in the top 1% mail letters, place ads in a variety of places, and also pick up the phone to communicate with the persons necessary to complete a transaction. This puts success in their own hands. They do not wait for the potential buyers and sellers to:

- Pick up the *newspaper*;
- Pick up the *right newspaper*;

- Pick up the *right newspaper in which they ran their ad*;
- Pick up the *right newspaper in which they ran their ad and turn to the right page*;
- Pick up the *right newspaper in which they ran their ad and turn to the right page and pick out their ad out of all the rest*;
- Pick up the *right newspaper in which they ran their ad and turn to the right page and pick out their ad out of all the rest and still be motivated to call them the next day*;
- Pick up the *right newspaper in which they ran their ad and turn to the right page and pick out their ad out of all the rest and still be motivated to call them the next day hoping they will be there to answer the phone*!

Can you see how many things, all of which are in the hands of other people, have to happen in order for you to be successful? What are you going to do if the person you need is in Japan when you run your ads, especially if you run out of ad money before he/she returns to read your ads? Mailing letters, advertising in the papers, Internet, and so on are all expensive and probably necessary. In fact they are so expensive you cannot afford them unless you are willing to match the effort and expense with person-to-person follow up!

IMPROVING VERBAL COMMUNICATION SKILLS

Competition forces us to constantly improve the media with which we communicate. Verbal presentations must be planned and rehearsed before they are used with the public. Written communications are also important because they can reappear later to haunt you.

Thousands of volumes are available from which you can secure effective communications skills. You should study one of these at least every six months. In all of your communications I suggest you have a minimum of two goals:

1. Don't make boring *presentations*! Use the *conversation* approach.

   Ask *questions*.

   Ask the *right* questions.

   Ask the right questions in the *right order*!

2. Don't ask for something illogical.

   Make your request *logical* and easy to immediately understand.

   Make it *convenient* for others to respond.

   Make it *urgent* so they will respond immediately.

   Make others *feel good* about responding to you.

Here are some suggestions for letters and telephone scripts to be used by intermediaries:

LETTERS TO SELLERS

Letters to potential sellers are often the initial effort made by intermediaries in building an inventory of businesses to sell. Be sure the letter is addressed individually to the person and marked *totally confidential* on the envelope. The first letter received by a prospect should never be longer than one page. Otherwise, it may be put away to be read later, which probably never occurs. Consider the following suggestions in your letters, but put it in your own words as you motivate potential sellers to respond to you:

Logical:

Buyers are looking for businesses like you own.

We have a buyer who is looking for _____ (the specific type of business owned by the person receiving the letter).

Many buyers want to move to your area.

This is a good time to consider selling.

We are successful! (possibly list some of your successes).

We are trained, certified, and so on.

The buyer will usually want all employees to remain, if they wish.

The buyer may even want you to stay, if you wish.

Convenient:

All you need to do is return the enclosed card.

I'll call you soon.

We do the marketing while you keep improving your business.

We assist you in each step of the process.

Urgent:

There are lots of buyers in the market.

Now is the time to consider selling your business.

Please tell your secretary to put me through to you when I call.

We are currently assisting hundreds of buyers in their search for the right business.

Feel Good:

Many owners want terms, but some get all cash.

Our communications are strictly confidential.

We are professional.

Selling your business is the ultimate reward for many years of work, sacrifice, and investment.

We will be discreet in all communications with you.

There was a time when I was willing to put my own letters in print for instruction purposes. I lost the motivation when a prospect handed me a letter from a competitor who had copied me word for word. It's really better for you to write your own and I'm sure it will be better than one I would give you.

TELEPHONE COMMUNICATION WITH SELLERS

Initial telephone calls to potential sellers are your second chance to make a professional impression. In all verbal communications, especially this one, it is important to secure as much information regarding the prospect while revealing as little as possible about yourself. Your statements must sound conversational and not like a salesperson. I try to make statements that leave the impression I am a good friend of the person for whom I am calling. Remember, no one other than the prospect (seller or buyer) should know the true intent of the call or you violate the statement of confidentiality promised in your first letter. These are some suggestions you may want to consider as you prepare and rehearse the script for this important call which is to follow an initial letter mailed by you:

Your statements: (*italic*)   Potential responses:
                                (light print)

1. *Hi, is _____ there? (Use first name only).*
2. May I say who is calling?

3. *Sure, this is _____ (your name).*

4. May I ask the nature of your call?

5. *Sure, it's personal, just tell him/her this is _____ (your name). He'll/she'll know.*

6. This is _____, may I help you? (Hopefully, the person for whom you called).

7. *Yes, this is _____, with _____ (your company name). We just received a card you dropped in the mail from a letter we mailed you about selling your business.*

8. *I assume you are the owner?*

9. Yes.

10. *Thank you for returning the card. I would like to visit by phone for a minute, and if we think appropriate, make an appointment to come visit in person.*

11. *What does _____ do? (Name of their company).*

12. Their response.

13. *Great! What are you going to do after you sell _____ (name of their company)? Alternative question: Why are you considering selling your business?*

14. *I would like to come see you to learn more.*

15. *Would _____ at _____ A.M./P.M., be fine with you?*

16. That's fine.

17. *Thank you! Did you write it on your calendar?*

18. *By the way, there are a lot of ways I can be helpful if you'll have some information available. If you'd like to know how to find out what your business is worth, please have some profit & loss statements, corresponding balance sheets, and tax returns handy.*

19. How much of this information do you need?

20. *Well, this visit doesn't cost you anything, so why not take advantage and have from 2 to 3 years, or more!*

21. I'll get what I can.

22. *Excellent, I'll see you on* _____ *at* _____ A.M./P.M. *Don't forget to write that on your calendar.*

MANAGING PROSPECTIVE RESPONSES

You may be thinking this script is not going to win any awards from my former college grammar instructors, and you're right. However, they are not winning any sales awards, either. Many actual conversations do not follow the script, so let's talk about what to do when someone won't follow your script:

1. When talking to the receptionist, using only the first name of the person you are calling leaves the impression you are on a first-name basis with that person.

2. When the first statement sounds right, you'll not hear this question more than 25% of the time. If you have your confidence at the proper level (but not arrogant), others will usually not feel the need to question you.

3. Don't be alarmed, just answer directly, but never give the name of your company! If they ask for the name of your company, simply say, *It's a personal call.*

4. The better you've done up to this point, the less likely you are to hear this question.

5. If you hear it, answer it and don't sound alarmed or upset. If they persist, say, *would you please tell him/her I'm on the phone. When I was asked to call, I was told to keep it personal!*

6. If they are not interested in the content of your initial letter, they will either not come to the phone or they'll tell you they are not interested. If they do talk to you, you've just learned they have more than a casual interest. The letter did its job and it's now up to you to properly cultivate that interest.

7. Be direct, but casual.

8. You need to talk to the owner and ascertain they are the only owner.

9. If there is more than one owner, you need to make arrangements to talk to all of them at the same time.

10. *The purpose of the initial letter was to prepare for this brief conversation. The only purpose of this conversation is to make an appointment to see them in person. This is not the time to sell the whole story, it's time to sell the appointment.*

11. They like to hear themselves talk more than listen to you. So, ask questions to get the information you need, but very few of them. Remember, you're only on the phone to get the appointment.

12. Listen and make notes. Do not interrupt them; the more they talk the more they are saying, "I like you."

13. Don't just talk, ask questions. The answer to this question is your first indication of how serious they are about selling.

14. Show an interest in them and they will want to know more about you, but not now!

15. You must train them to follow your lead and this is another lesson for them. Give them a specific time, but have more to suggest if necessary, one at a time.

16. If you sound confident and calm, they'll follow you.

17. Be sure this is a definite commitment on their part. Confirm it 24 hours in advance.

18. If they are not willing to provide specific information on the first visit, wait until they are willing to do so.

19. Be flexible, but firm in your request for specific information. If necessary, explain why it is needed.

20. Give them a carrot.

21. They are trying to cooperate.

22. Again, be specific about the appointment.

HANDLING TELEPHONE RESPONSES TO ADVERTISEMENTS

A prepared, often rehearsed script is helpful when potential sellers respond to your advertisement. Keep in mind the only thing you can sell over the telephone is an appointment to meet in person. If you are going to get that appointment you must immediately take control of the conversation without being obvious about it. While getting the appointment, your objective is to get as much information about the other person as possible while providing the minimum necessary to accomplish it.

Your statements: (*italic*)   Potential responses:
(light print)

1. *Good morning/afternoon, this is _____ (your name).*

2. Caller indicates they saw your ad which triggered this call to you about the possibility of selling their business.

3. *Thanks for calling. We have several ads, can you tell me which one you saw?*

4. They respond.

5. *I assume you are the owner.*

6. Yes.

7. *Let's talk a minute by phone, and if we think appropriate, I'd like to come visit with you in person.*

8. *What is the name of your company and what do you do?*

9. Their response.

10. *Great! What are you going to do after you sell* _____ *(name of their business)?* Alternative statement: *Why are you considering selling?*

11. *I would like to come see you to learn more.*

12. *Would* _____ *at* _____ A.M./P.M. *be fine with you?*

13. That's fine.

14. *Thank you! Don't forget to write it on your calendar.*

15. *By the way, there are a lot of ways I can be helpful if you'll have some information available. If you'd like to know how to find out what your business is worth, please have some profit & loss statements, corresponding balance sheets, and tax returns handy.*

16. How much of this information do you need?

17. *Well, this visit doesn't cost you anything, so why not take advantage and have from 2 to 3 years, or more!*

18. I'll get what I can.

19. *Excellent, I'll see you on* _____ *at* _____ A.M./P.M. *Did you write that on your calendar?*

Hopefully, you noticed a significant similarity in this script and the previous one provided for use when making a phone call to follow up on the original letter you mailed.

Consequently, I'll not repeat the explanations previously given.

The purpose of your question #3 is not to find out which ad they saw, as much as to get them accustomed to answering your questions and following your leadership. It is also useful in measuring the effectiveness of your advertising.

LETTERS TO PROSPECTIVE BUYERS

Initial letters to potential buyers are also successful tools used by many intermediaries. This is one of over 50 different steps provided in a later chapter to find buyers and sellers of businesses. It is important to include logical, convenient, urgent, and feel-good phrases and sentences as previously mentioned. Exhibit 5.1 is a letter that recently worked well for me.

Exhibit 5.1

Letter to Buyer Prospects

Date

Mr. Joe Prospect
P.O. Box 94
Golden, CO

Dear Mr. Prospect:

After many years as an intermediary, helping owners find qualified buyers for their profitable businesses, I find professionals like yourself are often interested in expanding their horizons by purchasing and/or merging with other businesses. Below are listed some excellent businesses for sale in your industry and/or geographical area:

The Top Sales Leader in Manufactured Housing in the Western United States. Also specializes in installation of mobile and modular homes as well as commercial build-

---

ings. Sales are in excess of $15,000,000 with profits in excess of $900,000. Twenty-one acres and a new two-story office building are also available.

Construction Company specializing in excavation and installation of utilities, road construction, and commercial paving. Sales are $1,857,000 with profits over $700,000. Real estate in use is also available.

Home Appliance, Electronics, and Furniture (two stores successfully owned by the same family for over 40 years) with sales of $1,500,000 and profits of $395,000. Five downtown buildings used in the business are available.

Commercial Electrical Contractor which has been family owned over 25 years with sales in excess of $2,250,000 and profits of $83,000. Real estate used by the company is also available.

Franchised Computer Training and Computer Sales company with sales in excess of $2,000,000, and growing rapidly. Real estate is leased.

Baskin-Robbins, Dunkin' Donuts, Blimpie's, and Bagel Store, one of only a few combo stores in the United States. Sales in excess of $500,000 and profits over $100,000.

Many of the buyers whom I've assisted do not necessarily buy in the same industry or geographical area in which they currently operate. Therefore, I have included some others on the back of this letter. We have many others— give us a call if you do not see what you want.

Additionally, our business valuation and appraisal services are performed by highly experienced professionals with appropriate licenses, certifications, designations, and affiliations.

If you have any interest in any of the above, please drop the enclosed card in the mail. We will be discreet in all communications with you!

Sincerely,

William W. (Bill) Bumstead, CBC, FCBI, BCB, LREB, PBC, LPI

CALLS TO PROSPECTIVE BUYERS

Initial telephone calls to potential buyers are important even though they may not return the card enclosed in the letter. Many will intend to mail the card, but just don't get it done. You will need to make minor adjustments to the following script when calling someone who did not return a card.

Your statements: (*italic*)   Potential responses: (light print)

1. *Hi, is _____ there? (Use first name only)*
2. May I say who is calling?
3. *Sure, this is _____ (your name).*
4. May I ask the nature of your call?
5. *Sure, it's personal, just tell him/her this is _____. He'll/she'll know.*
6. This is _____, may I help you? (Hopefully, the person for whom you called)
7. *Yes, this is _____ with _____ (your company name). We just received a card you dropped in the mail from a letter we mailed you about businesses we have for sale.*
8. *Thank you for returning the card. Can you tell me which of the businesses caught your attention?*
9. Their response.
10. *That's a good choice. We have a significant amount of information about that business, including several years of detailed financial history.*
11. *Being a business owner yourself, I'm sure you can understand the need for strict confidentiality in giving out*

this information. The owner of this business requires you first sign a nondisclosure statement, after which we can give you all the information you need.

Note: Some intermediaries feel it appropriate at this point to make a specific appointment for the potential buyer to come into the office for a personal visit. This obviously shows a greater degree of sincerity on the part of the potential buyer and gives the intermediary a more reliable impression of their abilities to pay for and manage the business. However, both potential buyers and intermediaries must manage their time well and the use of fax communications at this point may be appropriate.

12. *If you will give me your fax number, I'll fax this form to you immediately. What is that number: _____?*

13. Their response.

14. *As soon as you receive it, please fax it right back to me and we'll start the process of providing you with anything you need.*

15. Their response.

16. *Thank you, the form is on its way. I'll stand by to receive it back from you.*

17. Form is returned to you.

Call them back immediately.

18. *Thanks for returning the nondisclosure form so quickly. May I suggest we get the information to you in the following process:*

    (a)   *We have a brief profile of the business which includes the financial history for 1993, 1994, 1995, and 1996, as well as the price and terms offered. I will immediately fax or mail it to you. Would you rather it be faxed or mailed?*

19. Their response.

    (b) *After you review this information, we'll get back together on the telephone and continue to assist you. May I please have your other telephone numbers?*

Their response.

    (c) *Please feel free to call me at any time with any questions. I'll be glad to help you in any way possible! Thanks for your interest.*

This is your opportunity to earn a large fee by following up with all potential buyers in a timely manner. Never allow more than 72 hours to pass without communications with these individuals. Keep detailed records of all communications, both verbal, written, and electronic!

CALLS FROM BUYERS

The script you use when receiving calls from potential buyers responding to your advertising should be improved and rehearsed on a regular basis. Advertising is expensive, which means every one of these calls could represent from $50 to $100, or more, in expense as well as an opportunity to earn a large fee. If these calls are not handled professionally, it's like throwing a $100 bill out the window. Here are some suggestions; by now you should be able to do your own.

Your statements: (*italic*)   Potential responses:
                                        (light print)

1. *Good morning/afternoon, this is* _____ (*your name*).

2. Caller indicates they saw your ad of a business for sale.

3. *We have several ads in the market, can you tell me which one?*

4. Their response.

5. *Have you ever owned this type of business before?*

6. Their response.

7. *What about this ad caught your attention?*

8. Their response.

9. *Did you have any interest in any other ads?*

10. Their response.

11. *Actually, the business about which you called is an excellent choice.*

12. *We have a significant amount of information about that business, including several years of detailed financial history.*

13. *I'm sure you can understand the need for strict confidentiality in giving out this information. The owner of this business requires you first sign a nondisclosure statement, after which we can give you all the information you need.*

14. *If you will give me your fax number, I'll fax this form to you immediately. What is that number: _____?*

15. *As soon as you receive it, please fax it right back to me and we'll start the process of providing you with anything you need.*

16. Their response.

17. *Thank you, the form is on its way. I'll stand by to receive it back from you.*

As soon as you receive the returned nondisclosure form, follow up as outlined in the previous script. Don't give any information to any individual who does not first sign the nondisclosure form! These can be designed so they will only have to sign one form, one time, which can cover all future information received on future businesses.

THE TELEPHONE IS FOR MAKING APPOINTMENTS

Your success in *making deals* is in direct proportion to your ability to *make appointments* to ultimately communicate face-to-face with sellers, buyers, and the professionals they employ to help them make decisions. In these initial communications by letter and telephone you must develop a perfect balance between two opposing forces.

1. The need to provide adequate information to motivate others to make informed decisions and respond to your requests.
2. The restraint to not provide too much information which might confuse their ability to make limited decisions, one at a time.

Selling and buying businesses is like eating an elephant, there is a lot for sellers and buyers to digest. Keep your perspective and feed it to them a bite at a time. Initially, you want them to make a decision for an appointment, not sell or buy a business.

Think of your role as an intermediary like that of other professionals. Prospective clients must make an appointment with an attorney before either of them make any binding commitments. Patients must commit to an appointment with their doctor before any decisions are made regarding surgery. Your ability to develop trust in the importance of the initial face-to-face visit will become a significant factor in your proficiency in consummating transactions. Make constant efforts at improving these initial letters and telephone scripts and you will enjoy the increased responsiveness of potential sellers and buyers of businesses.

6

WORKING WITH SELLERS OF BUSINESSES

I am often asked to name the most important elements of success in working with sellers of businesses. It is difficult to limit the list, but here are some of those I find among the most successful in the industry.

QUALITY LISTINGS

A salable inventory of good quality listings from adequately motivated sellers would have to be at the top of the list. If you don't sell a reasonable amount of your inventory you are not making sufficient commissions and obviously not serving the needs of your sellers. You cannot sell a reasonable amount of them if they are not properly priced with adequate terms and conditions! You also cannot properly service an unlimited amount of listings. It is difficult to recommend how many listings can be handled by a single practitioner. I personally have 26 sole and exclusive listings as of this date and that's almost too many. I suspect the average is about half that amount, which is an additional reason to be sure they are all salable.

APPROPRIATE FEE STRUCTURES

In addition to what you earn from the businesses you sell, you should earn appropriate fees from those you don't sell! You must be paid for everything you do in this industry, not just commissions on business sales! A lot of professional services must be provided and if you provide them you must be paid for them. Most other professions are excellent examples. If an attorney takes your case, he/she will normally be paid by the hour. Win or lose, they are compensated for their services. If the arrangement is on contingency, a sizable retainer will be charged up-front to cover basic filing fees and other costs. The contingency will often require a 30%, 40%, or 50% success fee, and even more, be paid to the attorney.

An accountant is paid specific fees for services performed. Whether or not you like the taxes you may owe, he/she is paid. The physician is paid if you get well or if you die! All of these examples are appropriate and services provided in the valuation, buying, and selling of businesses are not any different! If you provide the following services, get paid for them up-front and/or as they are provided:

1. The business valuation is a must, and if you are involved in any way you should be paid for what you do. The chapter on marketing valuations shows you how to professionally participate in a variety of ways. Fees for valuations should be paid in full when they are ordered to

guarantee an opinion of value free of any relationship to fees.

2. Preparing and packaging a business for marketing requires a lot of expertise, time, and resources and should be paid for in a retainer. If the retainer is for this purpose, specifically note in the agreement it is paid up-front and is completely earned when packaging is completed.

3. Advertising and marketing costs are as regular as rent and should be considered another requirement for the retainer. Unless definite ads are agreed upon for the specific business involved, note in the agreement the retainer is a one-time payment, up-front, with no obligations for reporting or refunds.

4. Consulting is a major time consumer of the intermediary and a lot of it is requested prior to the signing of any agreement for fees. If consulting is provided prior to the signing of fee agreements, it should be paid for by the hour, just like other professionals referenced above.

These most important elements of the industry are covered in this chapter and are a part of your ability to successfully work with sellers of businesses. You have more objectives than just taking a listing when you have the first interview with the seller. Here are those I have found among the most successful professionals in the industry:

1. Business valuation, have you heard that before?
2. Sole and exclusive listing with a retainer paid up-front.

My research indicates that most large successful intermediary offices will not take any assignment from a potential seller if one or both of these are not part of the agree-

ment. As you found in previous chapters, these two requirements seem to be common among sellers who are most successful at securing the better prices for their businesses.

ALTERNATIVE ASSIGNMENTS AND
FEE AGREEMENTS

If the above two are not accomplished, how can you serve
the potential seller and get paid for your time? If you have
completed an interview with a potential seller, you have
invested hours and expenses. Are you going to walk away
without anything to show for this? A more important consideration is that this potential seller still needs some level of
professional services and would possibly be willing to pay
for them under different terms. Are you willing to consider
some income on their terms? A successful professional in
business sales and consulting indicates a large portion of his
annual income comes from these additional considerations.
In fact, he does not promote himself as an intermediary, he
is a *business sales consultant* and is certified by the Institute
of Certified Business Counselors as a CBC (certified business counselor). He does not have a single approach to selling businesses and considers it unrealistic to do so. He totally agrees with my first two objectives of a business
valuation and a sole and exclusive listing. However, if these
are not accomplished, he indicates he hates to not be paid for
his time and expenses invested and lose the opportunity to
secure other fees, as well as a potential listing in the future.

If you do not secure a sole and exclusive listing, some
other objectives may be worthy of your consideration. These
have been suggested to me by some successful sole practitioners who are not part of large offices which cannot deal
with irregularities:

1. What about an arrangement without an agreement for a commission? The seller simply pays for services as they are provided, with a retainer up-front equal to three months of the anticipated fees. Some of these services might include:

    (a) Business valuation, paid in full, up-front. The valuation could be a requirement for this optional arrangement!

    (b) Preparing the marketing package, paid by the hour.

    (c) Advertising, to be paid from the retainer which is replaced when depleted.

    (d) Taking calls from advertising and passing the prospects on to the seller, paid by the call.

    (e) Consulting with the seller on negotiations with potential buyers, paid by the hour.

    (f) Consulting with the seller regarding his selection of proper professional assistance in offers to purchase, closing activities, and so on.

2. A better arrangement might be a combination of the above agreements and a reduced commission or success fee if the business sale is consummated. The idea for this arrangement came from a seller who wanted to be sure the *consultant* was properly motivated to help secure a sale.

POSSIBLE BENEFITS FROM ALTERNATIVE ASSIGNMENTS AND FEE STRUCTURES

Those who are willing to work under these optional arrangements claim the following benefits to the *consultant*:

1. Business valuation fee, paid in full, up-front.

2. All services are obviously provided at a *profit*.

3. Advertising always carries the name and telephone number of the *consultant* who gains public recognition and other potential buyers and sellers who need their services.

4. Retained goodwill of the seller.

5. In about three months, most of these optional arrangements are changed into arrangements on the original terms of the *consultant* because the retainer has been consumed and the seller has gained respect for all of the things normally performed by an *intermediary*.

What is gained by the seller from participation in an *optional* arrangement:

1. A good education in the business marketing process.

2. A continued relationship with a reputable *consultant*.

3. Professional advice in each step of the process.

4. Assistance from the *consultant* in screening of potential buyers.

5. Confidentiality in the marketing process provided by the *consultant*.

6. Opportunity to deal direct with the potential buyers.

7. The opportunity to change to the *original* agreement offered by the *consultant* should he feel he does not have the time or expertise to handle the situation.

Regardless of your objectives, it is important that a proper agreement be used with those you serve. There is nothing more devastating than to come to the end of a successful assignment and then not be paid in full for your services because of an inadequate agreement.

Before you make an appointment for the original interview with a potential seller, put in writing your:

1. Preferred objectives
2. Alternative objectives, if you do not secure the preferred objectives

My advice is that you not reveal the entire list at once. Reveal them as you need them and are willing to accept them.

PROPERLY MOTIVATED SELLERS

Only properly motivated sellers will take you all the way to the bank! There is nothing more frustrating than to bring the best offer available in the marketplace to a seller and then be told the offer is not good enough, or they have changed their mind about selling. I firmly believe that all sellers must have motivations stronger than financial in order to consummate a transaction. When I approach a potential seller and am told: "I'll sell anything for the right price," I immediately know I'll probably never be able to get the right price because their only motivation is financial. The properly motivated seller must have firm reasons for selling in addition to financial. Some of these additional motivations are necessary to encourage the seller to accept the best offer available:

1. Retirement
2. Illness
3. Relocation
4. Burnout
5. Death of person running the business

6. Divorce

7. Disputes between partners, stockholders, and/or management

8. Physical stress

9. Financial stress

10. Mental stress

11. No children and/or other family members have an interest in the business

I begin looking for indications of these additional motivations from the beginning of the initial interview with a potential seller. If they are not obvious, I start asking questions that lead them to reveal their true motivations. The best motivations are confirmed when they pay the up-front retainer in addition to the business valuation!

Intermediaries should give serious consideration to not taking a listing unless all of the following ingredients are evident:

1. Business valuation

2. Proper seller motivation

3. Proper price and terms

4. Adequate length of listing to accomplish objectives

SEQUENCE OF EVENTS IN SELLING A BUSINESS

Working with sellers is not a simple task, but it becomes manageable and rewarding if you understand the sequence of events and don't try to short cut the process:

1. Find a potential seller.

2. Interview the potential seller.

3. Business valuation.

4. Sole and exclusive right to sell agreement, properly executed.

5. Prepare and package the business for marketing.

6. Institute the marketing process.

7. Find potential buyer(s).

8. Interview and qualify buyer(s).

9. Educate buyer(s).

10. Introduce buyer(s) to business and seller.

11. Motivate buyer(s).

12. Secure letter of intent (LOI) and/or offer to purchase (OTP).

13. Present LOI and/or OTP to seller.

14. Solve the problems!

15. Prepare for the closing.

16. Coordinate the closing.

17. Cash the check.

18. Purge and store the files for required amount of time.

19. Secure reference letters from both seller and buyer, as well as referrals.

20. Repeat the process!

EDUCATING SELLERS

It is important that you educate the potential seller in the important things to be accomplished in the selling of his/her business. I start this process in the initial interview, and will be sure to cover all of the following as soon as the proper agreements are signed between myself and the seller. *Be sure you do not overload the seller at first.* Use what is necessary of the following to get the business valuation and listing agreements signed in the first meeting, if possible. Then coordinate your activities and requests of the seller with your estimation of his/her ability to timely comply with your needs:

1. Sell myself and my company.
2. Allow the seller to sell himself and his business to me.
3. Stress the requirement of the business valuation.
4. Explain the sole and exclusive right to sell and security agreement, which gives me permission to assemble the important information, coordinate the marketing process, and collect fees provided in the agreement (Exhibits 6.1 and 6.2).
5. Confirm the need for agency agreement(s), corporate resolutions, partnership authorizations, and other agreements as required by law in the state.
6. Provide a questionnaire form which they can use to tell more about their business, which is helpful in the preparation of the marketing information (Exhibits 6.3 and 6.4).
7. Request supportive listing information that is unique to their business as well as financial statements, and so on (Exhibit 6.5).
8. Give an example of the confidentiality requirements and forms required of potential buyers (Exhibit 6.6).
9. Tell them the need of providing updates on assets offered in the sale, including inventory, and so on.
10. Ask them to make a list of anything that would be visible

Exhibit 6.1

Name of Intermediary Firm
Address of Intermediary Firm
Standard Business Listing Agreement

Intermediary Firm, hereinafter called Intermediary, agrees:
1. To use its best efforts to sell Owner's business and maintain confidentiality.
2. To present all written offers to Owner and register all persons receiving information regarding Owner's business.

Owner (includes individual, partners, stockholders, heirs, legal representatives & their assigns, all jointly & severally) agrees:
1. That it has the legal authority to list and sell the business and gives Intermediary the sole and exclusive right to sell the business and refer to Intermediary the names of any party who expresses an interest in the business, and that Intermediary's commission is a part of the proceeds from the sale and agrees to act as Intermediary's fiduciary and trustee, collect the funds, and pay Intermediary as agreed.
2. To provide Intermediary with accurate past, current, and future financial data, a list of assets to be sold and a legal description of any real estate listed, to cooperate with Intermediary, allow it to be present during negotiation, at the closing, and provide it with copies of all documents relating to offer(s) or to the sale.
3. That the sales commission shall be paid in cash upon closing and computed on the total sales price as though all assets were sold free and clear of debt regardless of the form of sale, and shall include, but not be limited to, cash, notes, leases, options to purchase, employment agreements, covenants not to compete, assumption of liabilities, and any other benefit which accrues to Owner as a result of the sale. If the business is a corporation the sales price shall include all current assets and any current assets removed by the Owner in anticipation of the sale shall be included. Commission on earn outs shall be paid as received, with the initial fee deducted from the first payments. The commission of real estate leased by the Owner in conjunction with the sale shall be computed on five years' gross lease amount.
4. To pay Intermediary its commission if the business is sold during the term of this contract, and to pay Intermediary its commission should this business or any other business or property in which Owner has an interest be sold to any buyer located directly or indirectly through the efforts of Intermediary, or its agents, during the term of,

(continued)

201

Exhibit 6.1 (continued)

or after the term, of this contract. All stockholders, officers, employees, partners, their family members, those who learn that the business is for sale during the term of this contract, and anyone connected to the business shall be considered to be located through the efforts of Intermediary.

5. That it has been apprised Intermediary is not a securities dealer and will not list or offer corporate stock for sale.

6. Not to circumvent this contract, and to accept the price and terms as stated, and that terms are accepted at Owner's sole risk and discretion, and to pay Intermediary its full commission when Owner sells, licenses, leases, transfers ownership, control of, refuses to sell at the listed or agreed upon price, or removes the business from the market prior to the expiration of this contract. Nothing in this contract shall prevent Owner from engaging in its normal business activity.

Both Owner and Intermediary agree:

1. That Owner will pay Intermediary an administrative fee of $____ herewith and a total commission based on the Owner's accepted selling price equal to ____% of the first one million dollars, plus ____% of the next million dollars, plus ____% of the next million dollars, plus ____% of the balance. The administrative fee shall not be refunded, but shall be deducted from any part of the commission which exceeds the minimum net commission to be paid of $____.

2. That both parties have chosen ____ County, ____ as proper venue for settlement of any disputes between the Parties relating to this agreement, and that the successful party shall be entitled to recover its costs, and that Intermediary has not guaranteed that the business will sell, or expressed an opinion of its value, and that except for portions which survive, this contract will terminate in one year at midnight on ___/___/___, and shall be renewable at Owner's option for an additional 12 months with no further administrative fee as long as no changes (other than sales price) are made to the contract, and that both Parties have read and understand this contract, and that the entire agreement is contained herein, and that no amendment or variation shall be valid unless in writing and signed by both Parties, and that any real estate shall be listed at Intermediary's home office by Intermediary.

The listed price, based on all assets free and clear of debt, shall be $_____, with terms: _____.

Form of Owner: ____ C Corp. ____ S Corp. ____ Proprietorship ____Partnership ____L.L.P.

Real Estate Included: _____

Name of Business	Telephone Numbers	Fax Number	E-mail Address

Business Physical Address	City	County	State	Zip Code

Mailing Address for All Correspondence

Name(s) of Owner(s)	Home Address	Telephone

Agreed to by Owner: Accepted by Intermediary:

By: _____ Individually & as its: _____ Its: _____
By: _____ Individually & as its: _____ Date: _____
Date: _____

Exhibit 6.2

Authorization to Release Information

To Whom It May Concern:

This form will serve as my authorization for you to release and furnish copies of the following to: _____.
If there is any charge for this service, please bill me accordingly. If there are any questions or problems regarding these instructions, please call me personally at: _____. The information I am authorizing you to release is as follows:

Thank you for all your cooperation and assistance!

_____
Seller   Date

Please have your local attorney compose this form for you.

Exhibit 6.3

Information Regarding Your Business

Ownership:

Type of Ownership: _____ Corporation (__S or __C); _____ Partnership; _____ Proprietorship; Other _____

If incorporated, give: Date: ___/___/___, State: _____

Total shares outstanding: _____

Name shareholders with number and percent of shares owned by each:

History:

Established: Date: ___/___/___; City: ____; County/State _____

Acquired: Date: ___/___/___; From: _____

Description of Your Business:

Description of Products and/or Services:

Describe Customer Base:

Projected sales this year: $_____   Next year: $_____

Number of current active accounts: _____

Terms of Credit: _____

Are revenues seasonal? If so, explain and indicate amounts for each season:

Major competitors and their market share in your trade area:

Reason business is being sold:

Strengths of the business:

Marketing Activities:

Marketing strategy and methods:

Describe basic advertising and promotional activities:

Employees and Management Team: # Full-Time: _____
                                     # Part-Time: _____

Job function   Tenure   Current wage   Last year wage   Benefits

Union Contract: ___ Yes ___ No   Contract expiration: ___/___/___

Describe pension or profit-sharing plan:

Describe any unfunded pension liabilities:

Total cost of unfunded pension liabilities:

Indicate desired status of owners after sale:

List Benefits of All Owners:

Item	*This Year* (12 mo. est.)	*Last Year* 19___	*Previous Year* 19___

(continued)

Exhibit 6.3 (continued)

Auto(s)
Travel & entertainment
Life insurance
Health insurance
Other (describe)
List all autos furnished to owners/officers/family:

Give the names, duties, and benefits, including wages of any family members who receive pay or benefits from the company:

Describe Economic Outlook:

List Assets Included in This Sale:

Please attach balance sheets, depreciation schedules, and P/L statements for the last four years, and list below all assets and liabilities not shown on financial statements:

Please list and include legal descriptions and photographs of all physical facilities used by the business:

Those Leased (Give terms of leases):

Those Owned (Indicate current values):

If recent appraisals are available, please enclose and indicate date(s) and value(s) above.

Provide Lists & Descriptions of Machinery, Equipment, and Vehicles, Not Included Above (Enclose photographs of major items and indicate which is leased, owned, and approximate ages, along with current values, life remaining, etc.). Please indicate and include appraisals with appraisal values where available:

Provide Lists and Descriptions of Office Furniture, Machines, Computers, Tools, and So On. (Indicate which is leased, owned, and approximate ages, along with current values, life remaining, etc.) Please indicate and include appraisals with appraisal values where available:

Provide Any Major Build-Out Expenses to Physical Facilities Which Have Not Been Depreciated:

Give the Development Costs of Any Patents & Copyrights:

What Would It Cost to Replace Your Current Inventory That Is for Resale?

What percent could be sold at retail?

What Would It Cost to Replace the Current Inventory You Have for Production and In-House Use?

What percent could be used or sold at retail?

Describe any substantial one-time expenses or extraordinary expenses incurred during the past four years:

Please list all legal actions pending and anticipated:

Listed Price: $____; Minimum down payment/terms: ____

What is the minimum cash price you would accept? $____

Has anyone expressed an interest in buying your business? (Indicate who and when):

(continued)

Exhibit 6.3 (continued)

Please Give Us Any Additional Information You Feel Would Be Helpful In Selling Your Business (Use back side of this page):

Is Business in Compliance With All Regulations?

1. Environmental
2. OSHA
3. IRS and local, county, and state taxing authorities
4. Zoning
5. Health regulations
6. Legal
7. Other

Exhibit 6.4

Demographics of Your Trade Area

Define Trade Area:

_____ County Demographics
(Name of Your County)
   Population:
   Elevation:
   Average temperature:
   Annual precipitation:
   Annual snowfall:
   Average humidity:

Major employers of your trade area:

Distance from your city (fill in below major cities within 250 miles of your location):

City	Miles	Population

Annual events of your city and trade area:

Major sight-seeing in your city and trade area:

Recreation opportunities of your city and trade area:

Major hotels and motels in your city and trade area:

Outstanding restaurants in your city and trade area:

Educational opportunities in your city and trade area:

Public transportation provided in your city and trade area:

Closest airport(s) to your city and trade area:

Major reasons for living in your city and trade area:

Additional business opportunities for _____
in your city and trade area: (name of your business)

For more information contact:

    Your city:

    County of _____:

    Area Chamber(s) of Commerce:

    Area economic development council(s):

    Convention and visitors bureau(s):

    Other:

Sportsman opportunities of trade area:

Indicators of economic growth in your city and trade area:

Opportunities for additional business for _____
in your city and trade area: (name of your business)

Miscellaneous:

Exhibit 6.5

Confidential Financial Worksheet

Item	Year: __	Year: __	Year: __	Year: __
Gross sales	____	____	____	____
(-) Cost of sales	____	____	____	____
(+) Other income	____	____	____	____
(=) *Gross profit*	____	____	____	____
(-) Total expenses	____	____	____	____
(=) *Taxable income*	____	____	____	____
(+) Depreciation	____	____	____	____
_____	____	____	____	____
(+) Interest	____	____	____	____
_____	____	____	____	____
_____	____	____	____	____
(+) Officer's compensation	____	____	____	____
_____	____	____	____	____
_____	____	____	____	____
_____	____	____	____	____
_____	____	____	____	____
(+) Miscellaneous	____	____	____	____
_____	____	____	____	____
_____	____	____	____	____
(=) *Net cash flow*	____	____	____	____

Current Assets			Year: __
Cash			____
Accounts receivable			____
Notes receivable-owner			____
Advances			____
Prepaid expenses			____
Inventory			____
Other assets			____
Subtotal	____	____	____
Fixed assets	(Cost)	(Market)	(Book)
Equipment	____	____	____
Real estate	____	____	____
Subtotal	____	____	____
Total assets	____	____	____
Liabilities			
Accounts payable	_____		
Accrued tax	_____		
Accrued pay r.	_____		
Short notes	_____		
Long notes	_____		
Notes/owner	_____		
Other liabilities	_____		
Total liabilities	_____		
Nt. W. Bk.	_____		

Notes to financial worksheets:

Exhibit 6.6

Nondisclosure Agreement

Date: _____   Page ____ of ____

To FAX#: (___) ____-____   Attn: _____   From: _____

I, the undersigned, for myself and/or on behalf of
_____, agree to retain in confidence and to
require my professional representatives and agents to retain in confidence any information provided to me by _____
(Consultant) in respect to any business represented for sale. Such "confidential" information might include financial statements, cost and
expense data, production data, trade secrets, secret processes and
formulae, plants and other properties, technology, marketing and customer data, sources of goods and materials, or the fact that the business is for sale. I also agree not to contact the Seller, Seller's employees, customers, suppliers, or lenders except through Consultant.

I understand that all information is provided by the Seller, and agree
to hold Consultant harmless from any claims resulting from its use.
I am apprised that Consultant is not a NASD registered Broker/Dealer
and offers no securities for sale.

I understand, unless otherwise apprised, that Consultant has a sole
and exclusive right to sell listing agreement and has been appointed
to be the sole Intermediary for the Seller. I agree to submit all communications with the Seller through Consultant, i.e., request for information, letter of intent, offer to purchase, etc.

I understand and agree that Consultant has a contract with the Seller
for payment of its commission and agree not to circumvent that contract, and that Consultant, having a financial interest, may obtain financial information about myself or the entity I represent through standard reporting agencies.

_____
Company Name (Please Print)   Address   City, State, Zip

_____
Individual Name (Please Print)   Office Phone   Home Phone

_____
Signature Individually and as its (Title)   Date

PLEASE COMPLETE, SIGN, AND MAIL TO THE ADDRESS
ABOVE, OR FAX TO: _____, THANK YOU!

to a potential buyer which would not be included in the assets of the sale.

11. Confirm in writing, with the proper forms required by the state, all real property included in the sale.

12. If the property used in the business is leased, get a copy and confirm in writing the terms of the lease that will be given to the buyer.

13. Explain the ingredients of the business profile which will be used in marketing and have the seller approve it by initialing each page of your rough draft before it is used.

14. Be specific about your marketing steps, such as:

    (a) Local advertising

    (b) Regional advertising

    (c) National advertising

    (d) International advertising

    (e) Use of the electronic media

    (f) Networking

    (g) Mailings

    (h) Cooperative agreements with other consultants

15. Stress that all offers will come through you and what forms they may take.

16. Explain the need of timely counteroffers.

17. Relate the possible need for investigative due diligence of the potential buyers.

18. Cover the issue of proper *third-party* representation of accountants and attorneys.

19. The escrow process should be understood by the seller.

20. The seller needs to be comfortable with how you will coordinate preparations for closing.

21. Closing procedures should be explained.

22. Explain the need for potential amendments to the original sole and exclusive listing and security agreement as the business financial picture changes.

23. Make sure the seller understands the advantages and disadvantages of stock versus assets sales.

HANDLING OBJECTIONS FROM POTENTIAL SELLERS

When you are professional in your first interview with sellers they will usually respond positively. However, there are some common objections you will see a thousand times when they are not yet properly motivated. Here are some answers:

1. "What's going on out there? I get one of those broker letters every week."

   Answer: Well, having a great business is like having the best yacht on the lake. Isn't it nice to have what everyone wants?

2. "Well, I'd sell everything I have for the right price."

   Answer: Surely there must be a greater motivation for selling. What about . . . ?

3. "I'll sell it myself and save a bundle in fees."

   Answer: You may sell it yourself, but after the interruption it will cause in your business, you'll probably lose more than you'll pay for professional help.

4. "I think I'll just wait until I'm 65 years of age, why now?"

   Answer: Timing is one of the most important aspects of selling anything. I can't predict the future, but I can tell you now is a great time.

5. "No one would ever pay me what I want for this business."

   Answer: You're probably right. If it's worth so much, maybe we'd better find you another one to buy.

6. "I'm making tons, why sell now?"

   Answer: When you're doing well is the time to sell.

7. "My real estate broker sold my house and did not charge me anything until it closed."

   Answer: First, let me say there are lots of excellent licensed real estate brokers in this business; in fact, you are looking at one. I and my company hold real estate licenses in every state that requires them in which we do business. Licensed real estate professionals are like licensed attorneys, accountants, and others. Just because you have a license doesn't mean you do everything in the industry the same way or charge the same fees for each service.

   Real estate professionals sell houses by putting a sign in your yard, placing the address and other information on the house in the MLS for the world to see, put a picture of the house in the local newspaper and tell everyone they know your house is for sale, as well as many other very effective things unique to selling houses. I don't think you want this done on your business. Your business is an income producing property in which effective commercial real estate persons are specially trained to use different techniques. However, they still often use for-sale signs and other ideas that violate the principle of confidentiality used in business sales.

   Because of their frustration with the ineffectiveness of these ideas, they have invited me to teach scores of seminars in the last few years to help them develop more effective ways of selling businesses. Those who use these professional business sales techniques are much more effective and charge the same type fees as business intermediaries. Actually, if a professional does not charge for a service, you can bet they either do not know how to provide it or do not plan to provide it in the first place.

I am currently working with a seller of a business who had engaged the services of a real estate professional. After spending $4,800 for a commercial real estate appraisal, they still did not know what to do about the values beyond land and buildings and did not know how to get it into the market where business buyers are found. A real estate professional, accountant, attorney, or anyone else can sell your business as well as me, just as long as they are:

1. Adequately trained
2. Properly licensed
3. Professionally certified
4. Perform all of the different techniques required
5. Have access to hundreds of prospects in the unique business buyer arena
6. Have the time and staff to do the job for you

The professional title we use is not important. I am certified as a:

1. Board certified business broker (BCB)
2. Certified business intermediary (CBI)
3. Certified business counselor (CBC)
4. Licensed real estate broker (LREB)
5. Licensed private investigator (LPI)
6. Professional business consultant (PBC), and others

What we do for you is much more important than *what we call ourselves*!

The list of objections from potential sellers could fill a book; however, most of them tend to fit into one of the above categories. Make you own list and learn to deal with them with fact and tact.

ADVANTAGES OF SELLERS USING INTERMEDIARIES

There are times potential sellers will need you to justify their need for your services instead of selling the business on their own. Some of the following have been helpful to me in these situations:

1. I have worked with buyers and their advisors for so many years I know the questions they will ask and the answers they want to hear. I use this expertise in preparing and packaging your business for the marketing process.

2. All selling is a numbers game and the number of potential buyers available to us is far greater because of our reputation in the industry, years of consistent advertising, networking possibilities, and many referrals.

3. You only have so many hours in the day and the ones you might spend in the selling process only take away from the operation of your business. The year you sell is the one in which you want to do your best at running the business. Let me do the selling and you keep growing your business.

4. Part of my expertise is knowing how to qualify potential buyers. I may initially talk to hundreds of buyers, but after I qualify them you may only need to talk to five of them.

5. Do you know how to get through the maze of the offer to purchase, escrow, and closing stages? My coordination of these activities alone is worth the fee you will pay me.

6. Confidentiality is one of the most important elements of the selling process. How are you going to make the initial communication with hundreds of people without revealing which business is for sale?

7. You do what you do best and I do what I do best. You need my professional knowledge in advertising, marketing, and handling other professionals who will become involved.

8. Have you ever heard of the *chase* in selling a business? You start chasing buyers and it will give them the idea you are desperate. They know the chase is my job and won't be alarmed.

9. I can negotiate on your behalf better than you. With an intermediary between you and the buyer, you have a buffer who can tell you all about the buyer without revealing sensitive things to the buyer about yourself.

10. Synergy is an important aspect of selling a business. You need every detail properly coordinated with the experience of a properly trained professional like me.

11. The best advantage offered by an intermediary is the experience gained from many years of consummating large numbers of transactions through solving problems on all sizes and types of businesses.

This list can be increased with many more ideas. Use your imagination and experience to make your own list. Review it often and be ready for questions without appearing alarmed, offended, or insecure.

SELLER-FINANCED TRANSACTIONS

A recent survey revealed most sales of closely held businesses are seller financed. Here are some of the reasons given:

1. All cash buyers often expect significant discounts of 25 to 30%.
2. Most buyers need terms and the number of potential buyers will be reduced by a large percentage (sometimes 50 to 75%) if terms are not offered.
3. Financial institutions are not in the market in significant numbers.
4. Did the seller pay the full price now being asked in cash?
5. Buyers have a better chance for survival with terms from the seller.
6. Possible tax advantages to seller.
7. Buyer needs a significant amount of cash for working capital and improvements or expansion.
8. Potential additional earn-out advantages can be offered to seller as part of terms.
9. Seller can receive good interest rates.
10. The business may not sell without seller financing.

INFORMATION AND DISCLOSURE REGARDING AGENCY RELATIONSHIPS

Almost every state requires specific statement(s) be signed by all potential sellers and buyers to be served by you. Many states provide and/or require the use of their own form(s). Consult your local attorney to be sure you have complied with this requirement.

SOLE AND EXCLUSIVE RIGHT TO SELL AND SECURITY AGREEMENT*

1. Identify the parties to the agreement and type of sale (asset, stock, etc.).
2. Identify the business.
3. List or refer to other lists of assets included in the sale to be attached.
4. List or refer to other listing of real property and/or leases to be attached.
5. List or refer to other lists of financial information to be attached.
6. Statement regarding any defects in any assets included in the sale.
7. Price and terms of sale.
8. Time and duration of the agreement.
9. Fees and retainer due agent and when due.

   List of all occurrences which trigger payments to agent.

   Seller will not attempt to transfer obligation to pay agent.
10. Duties and obligations of agent.
11. Obligations of seller should include:

    Legal capacity and authority of seller

    Seller's obligation to furnish information in a timely manner

    Agreement for agent being exclusive coordinator of offers, and so on

    Seller agrees to respond to all communications and offers in a timely manner

---

*Also see Exhibit 6.1.

Seller's obligation to not attempt to renegotiate fees

Agreement for agent to act as escrow agent, fiduciary, and trustee of all funds

All buyers are result of agent's activities and trigger fees due

Seller grants security interest to agent to ensure payment of fees

Statement regarding disputes and proper venue

Seller understands agent does not guarantee price

Contract binding on all parties of seller, joint and several

12. Indemnity granted to agent.

Contact your local attorney to draw this form for you in order to assure its compliance with all state laws. It is impossible to anticipate and cover all potential issues between the seller and intermediary in an agreement without making the document too long and confusing. A shorter, more easily understood agreement is always preferable. One of the best I've seen is one used by a very successful firm and an example is provided. Do not copy or use this agreement as printed. Consult your attorney!

CORPORATE RESOLUTIONS

Corporate resolutions confirm that a resolution has been adopted by the board of directors of said corporation, granting the power of the person signing all documents the right to do so. It is important that the date of this document either be the same as, or precede, the date on the listing agreement. Contact your local attorney to prepare this form for you.

PARTNERSHIP AUTHORIZATIONS

Partnership authorizations confirm that a quorum (or whatever is required in the state) of the partners voted to grant authorization to the person signing all documents the right to do so. It is important the date of this document either be the same as, or precede, the date on the listing agreement.

Contact your local attorney to prepare this form for you.

7

PACKAGING BUSINESSES FOR THE MARKETING PROCESS

I recently completed a business valuation for an up-scale jewelry store that specializes in the sale of large diamonds. On the initial visit to the store while waiting for the availability of the owners, I was impressed with the professional manner in which *consultants* were presenting stones to potential purchasers and found some good lessons for our industry. The counter on which they were making their presentations was definitely not cluttered. The stones were shown one at a time and carefully placed on a velvet pad with nothing else in immediate view. There were no two stones alike. Each had its own *story* which was carefully shared with the customer. The stones were even placed in loose potential mountings to capture the imagination of the final look.

The presentation skills of marketing a business create important first impressions before the potential purchaser actually views the business. Each business has its own unique story which must be presented in an uncluttered manner with adequate emphasis to make the potential purchaser feel this is the only one under consideration, at least at the moment. The imagination of the buyer must be captured in a way that helps him/her create a mental image of the final look with them as the new successful owner.

THREE IMPORTANT CONSIDERATIONS

The proper packaging of a business is the work of a professional, actually an artist, just like the diamond consultant. There are at least three important elements you should consider:

Confidentiality requirements of the seller

Protection of the fees ultimately due the intermediary

Use of the finest professional presentation skills in telling the story

1. Maintaining confidentiality is not only important in protecting the identity of the business and owner, it also contributes to the curiosity of the potential buyer who hopefully cannot wait to comply with the requirements in order to receive information. If properly written, the nondisclosure agreement also helps professionals collect appropriate fees and provides some legal protection for everyone involved. This should get everyone's attention and guarantee compliance. Never give the identity of any business to anyone who has not previously signed the agreement! It could be composed to allow potential buyers to sign only one form one time, even though they may

request information on several businesses at different times. Some professionals recommend one on each business to create a better *paper trail*.

In 26 years of selling businesses I've never encountered a serious problem with confidentiality because I stick to my rule. Real buyers will understand the need and readily comply. Those who will not comply do you a favor by refusing to do so. This refusal keeps them from wasting your time on other issues with which they will not comply. Some ideas for this agreement are found at the end of this chapter (Exhibit 7.1). A few sellers will want additional confidentiality requirements. If so, the marketing effort may be more difficult and buyers will become frustrated if this issue is not kept practical.

2. I don't know of any one single action or verbiage that will ultimately guarantee the payment of all fees with no questions asked by anyone. Occasionally, there will be someone who will decide to spend $50,000, or more, in legal expenses in an attempt to avoid the payment of earned success fees of $100,000, or more. If professionals properly prepare all paperwork, those trying to avoid fees will, hopefully, end up spending more than they are trying to avoid.

   I previously shared some ideas to consider including in the sole and exclusive right to sell and security agreement to protect these fees. The nondisclosure and marketing package are other opportunities to include self-protection of not only professional fees, but liability for information and actions of third parties.

   Other agreements in which there should be similar protection of professional fees and liability are:

   • Professional's disclaimer attached to the purchase agreement(s), signed by all parties.

- Professional's disclaimer attached to the closing documents, signed by all parties.

If professionals end up in litigation with properly written and signed documents, it will be more difficult for someone else to convince the jury when his/her signature appears on several documents agreeing to pay for services provided.

3. The story of the business must be told with the finest communication tools available. This is a very important part of any marketing effort. I remember a friend who once called to sell me some government bonds he owned. I asked him when he bought them and he replied: "I didn't buy them. Some bond salesman sold them to me and you should have heard his story." We are fortunate to have so many wonderful communication aids and we are fools if we don't use all of them as appropriate. Our best tool is our own person-to-person communication skills. Unfortunately, every potential buyer is not in personal communication with us, especially initially, which creates the need for other communication tools.

THREE POTENTIAL STAGES OF THE PRESENTATION PROCESS

The collection of forms presenting the business is often called the *profile* or *package*, which will include the printed pages of information to be handed out, mailed, faxed, sent through e-mail, and other mediums. To make it easy to comply with confidentiality requirements, this information is divided into three groups, with specific suggestions included at the end of the chapter:

The preliminary profile is one single page with very brief information which does not identify the business. It is normally not necessary to sign the nondisclosure agreement to receive this preliminary profile, although some intermediaries require it (Exhibit 7.2).

The business profile identifies the business and gives adequate information usually requested by potential buyers to allow them to make an appointment to visit the business and owner(s). Execution of the nondisclosure agreement is required to receive a copy of this business profile (Exhibit 7.3).

The master profile is available only at the office and includes all the information available on the business, usually in a loose-leaf notebook form. This is never removed from the office, but potential buyers may view it at any time and request copies of individual pages. The nondisclosure agreement should have been signed already; it is required when viewing this master profile (Exhibit 7.4).

ADDITIONAL PRESENTATION AIDS

1. A notebook of glossy color prints with appropriate captions is an excellent tool to give positive mental images to potential buyers. There is usually only one copy, which is kept in the office.
2. Slide presentations are even better, but require specific equipment which is not always available. Consequently, this is usually only available in the office.

3. Portable computers allow very professional presentations with photographs, graphics, and sound and are easy to take anywhere.

4. The most successful intermediary firm I know uses professionally prepared videos which may be sent to any serious potential buyer anywhere. They have a full-time video staff which edits and makes quality presentations with video, sound, and graphics.

5. Another successful firm combines many of the above into a coordinated presentation of printed materials, poster boards, slides, videos, and so on, all organized and presented uninterrupted to impress the potential buyer.

    Obviously, some of these require significant expense and should not be used unless up-front retainers allow for them, and at a profit! If sellers understand the importance of this type of representation, they will be happy to pay for it.

SUGGESTIONS FOR PRESENTATION FORMS

The following (Exhibits 7.1 to 7.4) are outlined suggestions for ideas to be included in the above-referenced presentations. Use your imagination and communication skills to prepare attractive and enticing collections of information which properly represent the type of business you are selling.

Exhibit 7.1

Nondisclosure Agreement (Also see Exhibit 6.6)

Parties to the agreement:

Potential buyer agrees:

To keep all information totally confidential

Not to disclose business is for sale

Not to contact the seller directly, unless through intermediary

Not to attempt to circumvent agreement between seller and intermediary

To allow investigative due-diligence and credit checks by intermediary and/or seller

To provide information as requested

To hold intermediary harmless for all information provided by seller or third parties

To submit all communications to seller through intermediary

Not to use information received for competitive purposes

Potential buyer acknowledges:

Agency relationship of intermediary with seller and with himself/herself

Type of sale offered: asset, stock, merger, and so on

Licensing status of intermediary (normally, not a securities offering)

Whether individual buyer, corporation, partnership, and so on

Statement regarding EPA requirements

Signature and specific information regarding potential buyer

Exhibit 7.2

The Preliminary Profile

Type of business: _____

Brief description of business:

Brief four-year history of sales, expenses, and recast cash flow:

Brief description of recast assets, liabilities, and net worth:

Asking price and description of terms offered:

Disclaimer of intermediary regarding information provided by seller and third parties:

Requirements for confidentiality:

Identification of intermediary:

Exhibit 7.3

The Business Profile

This profile can contain any number of pages, depending upon information available and the appropriate uses of it.

The first page could be the same format as *the preliminary profile* with the possible addition of the identification of the name and location of the business. Some intermediaries still do not include any identification of the business.

The next few pages should be a precise presentation of the information gathered from the seller in the form *information regarding your business,* which was introduced in the previous chapter.

The next information included should be that provided by the seller in *demographics of your trade area,* which was introduced to you in the previous chapter.

After careful inspection, the complete financial statements and tax returns (with appropriate recasting) for the previous four years could be attached, or a statement could be included making them available to serious potential buyers.

This profile should end with statements regarding the exclusive right of representation of the intermediary and the requirements of confidentiality.

Be sure to include adequate information needed to conveniently contact the intermediary.

Exhibit 7.4

The Master Profile

This should include identical copies of previously described:

> Nondisclosure agreement
> The preliminary profile
> The business profile

Some of the other items in the profile could include:

Corporate resolution or whatever is appropriate
Authorization to release information
All financial information
Original copy of information regarding your business as
    provided by seller
Original copy of demographics of your trade area as
    provided by seller
Furniture, fixtures, equipment, and machinery lists as
    provided by seller
Inventory list(s) as provided by seller
Equipment lease(s)/contracts
Real property information as provided by seller
Appraisals/valuations
Lease/rental agreement(s) as provided by seller
Leasehold improvements list(s)
Franchise/distributor agreement(s)
Notes/mortgages
Insurance policies

(continued)

Exhibit 7.4 (continued)

Service contracts
All advertising agreements
Personal property tax returns
Real estate tax returns
FICA (941-Qt.), FUTA (940-Ann.), SUTA (C3-At.), and
    other appropriate returns
Photographs
Slides
Videos
Maps of area
Testimonials
Client list(s)
Brochures, etc.
Marketing materials
Industry *sizzle* information
Union information
Traffic counts of area
Landlord intent to lease to buyer
Certificate of good standing from state comptroller or
    appropriate agency
Letter of good standing from the state tax office
Search of liens at the county and state levels

This is not intended to be a complete list, but rather an indication of the types of information required. Also, be aware that everything in the operation of the business does not have to be in this profile. All information should be updated every 120 days!

8

WORKING WITH BUYERS OF BUSINESSES

Properly motivated buyers, financially capable of consummating a deal, are obviously essential in any transaction. Without them you have no sale, merger, or anything. Some professionals in the industry are now working exclusively with potential buyers and reporting encouraging success. At the end of this chapter you will find some suggested ingredients that could be included in a buyer representation fee agreement.

Most intermediaries who work with both sellers and buyers report the numbers of their potential buyers are far greater than their list of sellers. Most advertising will usually generate more calls from potential buyers than potential sellers. A large intermediary firm reports less than 400 sole and exclusive listings and a current potential buyers list in excess of 10,000. If these percentages are reasonably representative of the industry, and I'm not able to prove they are, then why are there so many more buyers than sellers in the market?

QUESTIONABLE BUYER CHARACTERISTICS

The feeling among some consultants that all buyers are liars is not necessarily true; however, many of them are not initially prepared to make an educated purchase. Buying is an educational process and many of them enter the marketplace before they have determined what they really want or can afford. Most of them are forced to change their minds because what they want is not available. To some degree, buyers are like single people looking for the perfect mate. Regardless of what you think the ideal match needs to be, once you decide to make the big leap you can only choose from those currently available.

Because of this uncertainty of working with buyers, it is important you determine their sincerity and financial capabilities immediately, or as soon as possible. It may be a complete waste of your time if you don't require verification of their financial resources as a part of your second meeting with them. In addition, some consultants are doing background checks which we call *investigative due-diligence*. I suggest an LPI (licensed private investigator) should do investigative work for sellers, buyers, and their intermediaries before they enter into any contractual agreements on potential transactions. If buyers have a history of being corporate raiders or other questionable tendencies, it's important to know it up-front.

Anytime a buyer is hesitant about providing information, you should consider this a red flag and become suspicious about his/her intentions. I once had a buyer storm out of my office when I requested he fill out a questionnaire during our first meeting, mainly because he was required to furnish his driver's license number. When he later called back to see if I had changed my mind, I said I had definitely changed my mind. My decision was I would never meet with him again. Working with potential buyers can be an enjoyable and financially rewarding experience. The previous comments are only provided to encourage a higher degree of professionalism in the process.

THE ANATOMY OF SERIOUS BUYERS

There are some positive traits of potential buyers which will provide early signs of their sincerity:

1. Current and/or previous business success
2. History of buying, improving, and selling businesses
3. Adequate financial resources
4. Reasonable expectations regarding:

    Price

    Operating capital needed

    Time involved in owning a business

    Energy expended in operating businesses

    Tax benefits

    Leverage expectations and financing requirements

    Tax advantages

    Inflation

    Return on investment

5. Spirit of independence
6. Sense of urgency
7. Adequate decision maker
8. Pride and prestige

9. Reasonable expectations of risk involved

10. Desire to build an estate

11. A dreamer

12. Good person-to-person skills

13. Manifests leadership qualities

14. Responds to requests in a timely manner

15. Appreciates professionalism

16. Asks lots of intelligent questions

17. Looks for things to improve in businesses

This is certainly not an exhaustive list, but will give you the idea of the type of buyer who will take you to the bank.

THE SEQUENCE OF EVENTS IN SUCCESSFUL BUYER RELATIONSHIPS

The logical steps to a successful relationship with potential buyers could include the following:

1. Locating potential buyers. (See Chapter 4.)

2. Initial interview which produces adequate information.

3. Signed agreements(s) that produce the proper agency relationship.

4. Possible sole and exclusive right to do a buyer search.

5. Locate suitable option(s) for the buyer.

6. Present the option(s). Be sure a nondisclosure agreement is signed.

7. On-site presentation of the business and seller.

8. Offer to purchase or letter of intent.

9. Present offer to seller.

10. Solve the problems.

11. Turn the offer into a binding contract.

12. Preparations for closing.

13. Closing.

14. Purge/store files for proper time.

INITIAL BUYER INTERVIEWS

During the initial buyer interview it is important to cover all of the following (if appropriate at that time) depending upon the response of the buyer:

1. Explain agency relationship options approved in your state and have them sign the appropriate form acknowledging their relationship to you.

2. The confidential buyer questionnaire (Exhibit 8.1) is essential and should be completed early in the meeting.

3. Tell the buyer that he/she is to bring copies of financial statements as a requirement for the second meeting. If these are not available, provide forms for this use. Copies of standard forms can be secured from any financial institution.

4. After the questionnaire is completed and additional questions answered, you should have an idea of listings in your inventory that may potentially meet the buyer's needs.

5. Show him/her the preliminary profile(s) on appropriate listings; the fewer the better.

6. Have him/her sign the nondisclosure form.

7. Provide the business profile on the one(s) he/she may choose.

8. Offer access to the master profile(s), if necessary.

9. Discuss and make appointment(s) for on-site visit(s).

IT'S TIME TO GET SERIOUS

After the on-site visit, use the follow-up questionnaire (Exhibit 8.2) and conversations with the buyer to determine the appropriateness of the business(es) for his/her requirements. Hopefully, it will be time to utilize the following steps toward a purchase:

1. Offer to purchase

2. Binding contract

3. Escrow

4. Closing

5. Congratulations!

I heard of an intermediary who would put some buyers on his *thief list*. This list is composed of buyers who will only purchase if they are convinced they have made a deal that is at least 25%, or more, below the legitimate market value. When this becomes obvious to me, I'll usually find a humorous way to ask them if they would like to be on my special list of buyers who will not pay market price, but want to be notified when a business can be *stolen*. I make them aware there are a lot of names on the list. So, when I call they must return my call immediately, be ready to write a binding contract within 24 hours, and have access to ready cash to close the deal quickly. Sometimes, not very often, this will shock them into realizing they need to do a personal reality check.

Some assistance in handling objections of potential buyers is found in Exhibit 8.3.

WORKING EXCLUSIVELY WITH A BUYER

The professional buyer search is an opportunity for you to work for the potential buyer under a sole and exclusive acquisition agreement (see Exhibit 8.4). Under this arrangement, specific assignment(s), terms, and agreement(s) are made on behalf of the buyer for definite fee provisions. Properly executed agency agreements with the buyer and potential sellers will assure the proper fee(s) are received. This allows you to educate the buyer about the process you will use to find a specific business in a definite price range and geographical area. An appropriate retainer should be included to cover expenses in the initial stages and written progress reports may be required of the intermediary.

COORDINATING THE OFFER PROCESS

One thing for sure, you will be more certain you are working with a serious buyer who has the resources to complete a transaction. This can be a wonderful experience, try it!

It is imperative that the consultant be prepared to stay in charge and coordinate the important steps involved in preparing and presenting the appropriate documents to the seller to purchase his/her business. For the purposes of this chapter, we will address activities involved only in an asset purchase. Please notice I said *coordinate*, I did not say prepare the documents. Even if the intermediary is a licensed attorney, these should be prepared by an independent third party, another licensed attorney. Common items included in these documents are provided at the end of the chapter. Please note I am only offering suggested lists of items. Complete documents should be prepared by properly licensed professionals!

Some buyers initially use a letter of intent (Exhibit 8.5) which may include language definitely informing the seller this is not a binding agreement. Others may use an offer to purchase agreement (Exhibit 8.6) with language reflecting the binding effect of the agreement. Some will come straight to the table with an asset purchase agreement which will possibly include all of the terms and conditions actually used at the closing. I have seen these documents range from as few as 10 pages, up to as much as 200 pages, or more. Be sure a disclaimer (Exhibit 8.7) and hold harmless statement, ideally a separate form, is included to protect the potential exposure of professionals involved. Your coordination should include other items such as:

1. Normal prorations (Exhibit 8.8).
2. Items to be accomplished prior to closing (Exhibit 8.9).
3. Counteroffers (Exhibit 8.10).

The following sample forms (Exhibits 8.1–8.10) may be helpful as their attorney prepares the forms used with your potential buyers and sellers.

Exhibit 8.1

Confidential Buyer Questionnaire
(Used during the initial interview with intermediary.)

Name: Phone(s):

Address:

Current occupation: How long:

Previous business experience:

Best skills/interest: Is resume available:

Who will assist in your decision:

How soon do you plan a purchase:

Why do you want to own your own business:

What types of businesses will you consider:

Geographic area(s) desired:

How will you participate in day-to-day operations:

Annual sales volume desired:

Annual net cash flow desired:

Operating hours/days desired:

Down payment you have available:

Working capital available:

Collateral available:

How will you finance purchase:

Other information:

The undersigned certifies the above is true and correct and grants permission for normal credit and investigative checks to be performed by the intermediary, if requested by seller(s) of business(es) on which information has been requested. Sellers require you to keep strictly confidential

(continued)

241

Exhibit 8.1 (continued)

any information given to you and understand communications will be handled exclusively through:
_____ (name of intermediary).

State Drivers License #: _____

Social Security Number: _____

Full Name: _____

Address: _____

Telephone Number(s): _____

Potential Buyer's Signature: _____ Date: _____

Initials of Intermediary: _____

Exhibit 8.2

Buyer Follow-Up Questionnaire

Business Visited:

Business Visited by:

Date of Visit: Accompanying Intermediary:

1. Please give your opinion of the physical appearance of business operations:
2. Relate your opinion of the appearance and quality of real property used by business:
3. What is your opinion of the quality and adequacy of the furniture, fixtures, equipment, and/or machinery used in the business?
4. Please share your reaction to the financial performance of the business operations:
5. How do you rate the accuracy of the financial information provided?

6. Please list five things you think you could improve in the business:
7. Do you have a continued interest in this business?
8. List any additional information and assistance you need regarding this business:
9. If this business does not meet your requirements, please tell us how we may better select another for your consideration:
10. We appreciate any additional comments:

Signature of Potential Buyer: _____ Date: _____

Initials of Intermediary: _____

Exhibit 8.3

Handling Objections of Potential Buyers

1. "I need to talk to my 'advisors' before I proceed."
   Response:

   "Professional advice can be very helpful if the professional used is properly trained, certified, and has adequate experience in the specific area you have questions. For instance, I'm not the one to give you accounting, tax, or legal advice (third parties are more appropriate). In fact, I'll be glad to talk to these professionals with you. Or if you wish, feel free to have them contact me directly."

2. "The seller is asking too much."
   Response:

   "What do you feel is reasonable? Let's open the door with a reasonable offer."

3. "Too much is asked for a down payment."
   Response:

   "What do you feel is reasonable? Let's open the door with a reasonable offer."

(continued)

Exhibit 8.3 (continued)

4. "I cannot make a decision now."
   Response:

   "Is there a particular area of concern with which you would like me to assist you?"

5. "There are some things that concern me about that business."
   Response:

   "No business is perfect, let's make a list of the things needed for improvement."

6. "Let's see what else you have available."
   Responses:

   "Maybe I've covered this information too fast."

   "Have you made a list of the things you like about this one?"

   "Perhaps we should consider another business."

   "Can you be more specific about your needs/wants/ dreams?"

Note: Determine if you are dealing with: stalls, objections, or facts, then handle each accordingly!

Exhibit 8.4

Buyer Acquisition Agreement

Parties to the Agreement:

Sole and Exclusive Agreement: State-required agency agreement should be attached.

Purpose of the Agreement: Statements regarding specific assignment(s) given to intermediary with confidentiality requirements regarding handling of information provided by buyer and no purchase guarantee by buyer or successful search by intermediary. Intermediary is directed to coordinate activities of all professionals involved with buyer.

Buyer understands that consultant also represents other buyers and sellers on different issues.

Primary Term of Agreement: There should be specific dates with provisions for continuation and/or amendment, if appropriate.

Fees Payable to Consultant: Provisions may be made for an up-front retainer by the hour, assignment, and/or commission or success fee.

Specific Requirement(s) For Consultant Fee to Be Earned (how and when paid): There should be a 24/36 month protection period for consultant on all businesses shown to buyer.

Definition(s) of Specific Terms Relating to Earning of Fee(s), such as *purchase,* and so on.

Buyer Warranty of Available Funds and Capabilities, including but not limited to professional fees, down payment, prorations at closing, new financing, inventory, accounts payable, closing costs, start-up expenses, operating capital, and so on.

Statements Regarding Valuation(s) and/or Investigative Due Diligence:

Buyer Statements of Indemnification and Hold Harmless of Consultant:

Buyer Agreement to Not Disclose Proprietary Information Received From Sellers:

All Parties of Buyer Bound by Agreement:

Other Provisions:

_____   _____
Buyer   Date   Consultant   Date

Exhibit 8.5

Letter of Intent to Purchase

Intent to purchase certain assets:

Parties:

Assets to be purchased:

Purchase price and terms:

Expected conduct of business by seller until closing:

Closing conditions:

Confidentiality:

Timing of binding offer to purchase to follow:

Timing of closing:

Fees to be paid to Intermediary and other professionals:

Expenses of process:

Binding effect:

Other considerations:

Signatures:

Exhibit 8.6

Offer to Purchase Agreement

Asset agreement:

Parties:

Assets to be purchased:

Purchase price and terms:

Inventory considerations:

Taxes and prorations considerations:

Escrow:

Possession and closing:

Fees paid to intermediaries and third parties:

Warranties of seller:

Acknowledgments of buyer:

Timing of this agreement:

Defaults:

Additional terms and considerations:

Addendum(s):

    Inventory list(s)

    List(s) of assets

    Disclaimer(s)

    Items to be prorated

    Items to be accomplished prior to closing and by whom

    Corporate resolution(s)

    Partnership authorization(s)

Consult your legal counsel.

Signatures:

Disclaimer of Consultant/Broker/Intermediary

Parties:

Business:

Agreement that function of consultant has been fulfilled:

Seller and buyer acknowledge responsibility for their own investigation and interpretation of all information, and so on:

Seller and buyer hold consultant harmless for all information provided:

Seller and buyer acknowledge proper agency relationship(s) of consultant:

Seller and buyer acknowledge advice from consultant to seek independent third-party legal, tax, and financial advice:

Signatures:

Exhibit 8.8

Items to Be Prorated

Items to be prorated:	At closing	Outside of closing
Parties:		
Business:		
Items to be prorated:		
Insurance		
Telephone bills		
Telephone equipment lease(s)		
Utility bills		
Utility deposits		
Rent(s)		
Rent security deposit(s)		
Real property payments		
Taxes		
Other deposit(s)		
Alarm payment(s)/lease/rent/deposit(s)		
Equipment payment(s)/lease(s)/rent(s)/ deposit(s)		
Vehicle payment(s)/lease(s)/rent(s)/deposit(s)		
Maintenance contract(s) payment(s)/deposit(s)		
License(s) fee(s)/deposit(s)		
Advance revenues		
Advance payments		
Work in progress		
Wages/commissions/bonuses		
Retirement plans		
Payroll taxes		
City/county/state/federal taxes		
Accounts receivable		
Factoring		
Accounts payable		
Advertising		
Other		

This list is provided as a courtesy of _____
and is not intended to be a full and complete disclosure of all
items to be prorated. Additional items may be added later,
however, the above records the intentions of the seller and buyer
on this date.

Signatures:

Exhibit 8.9

Items to Be Accomplished Prior to Closing

Items to Be Accomplished	Date to Be Accomplished	By Whom
Set closing date		
Remove contingencies		
Arrange financing		
Payment of escrow fees		
Certified check(s) for closing		
Certify inventory		
Certify equipment		
Instructions for escrow agent		
Apply for new licenses/ permits		
Transfer utilities		
Lease assignment(s)		
New banking accounts		
Transfer franchise(s)/ distributorship(s)		
Advertising responsibilities		
Name change		
Logo change		
New stationery/printing/etc.		
Transfer insurance		
Title commitment(s)		
Signatures:		

Exhibit 8.10

Counteroffer

Parties:

Business:

I/we accept all of the terms and conditions of the offer to purchase and sale of assets agreement dated _____ , except as follows:

Should the ____buyer, ____ seller fail to accept this counteroffer on or before _____ o'clock ___A.M., ___ P.M. on _____ , 19___, this counteroffer is revoked and the deposit will be returned, in full, to buyer. The intermediary is authorized to deposit the earnest money deposit on behalf of the parties to this agreement with the escrow agent in a timely manner. Receipt of a copy of this counteroffer is hereby acknowledged by all parties.

Signatures:

_____		_____	
Seller	Date	Buyer	Date
_____		_____	
Seller	Date	Buyer	Date

9

MAINTAINING CONFIDENTIALITY

It is virtually impossible for the owner to sell his/her own business and maintain confidentiality in the process. Someone has to serve as an intermediary with the ability to communicate with potentially interested buyers without revealing the identity of the owner, name, specific address, or telephone number of the business.

THE NEED FOR CONFIDENTIALITY

If employees find out the business is for sale they will potentially become insecure in their relationship with management and begin to seek employment elsewhere, often with competitors, in order to protect the financial security of their family. They could also take less interest in their work and even sabotage the owner and/or reveal company secrets to competitors. If it is necessary or inevitable that some key employees will either find out, or it is necessary to inform them of the impending sale, a key employee retention agreement with these key employees may be considered to ensure a smooth transition to the new owner. The loss of key employees may diminish the value of the business to the potential buyer.

Suppliers will lose confidence in their ability to collect money due them and may even begin to seek other potential distribution possibilities for their products and services. This could be devastating to the business when it needs to look its best.

Bankers always become nervous when they hear anything about a business that could affect their collateral concerning the gross sales or cash flow which secure their payments. The year a business is sold is when it needs to display the ability to grow and finance that growth.

Specific customers, clients, and the public in general need to remain free of any fear or doubt that the business will remain capable of standing behind products and services previously delivered. In order to retain their confidence of continued business it is important they never hear anything to make them feel they are at risk!

The media is constantly in search of anything potentially sensitive or damaging. It would be bad enough if any of the above referenced found out which business was to be for sale and much worse if they shared it with newspapers, radio, television, and so on.

Intermediaries provide a great service by assisting in the communications and negotiations of sellers and buyers after they have been properly introduced and everyone involved has executed documents to protect confidentiality. The professional way they handle the identity of these principals prior to meeting each other is even more important, and obviously something the principals cannot do for themselves.

INTERMEDIARIES MUST FIRST SELL THEMSELVES

Consequently, the best thing intermediaries can do is sell themselves to the public as the place to go when someone has an interest in buying or selling businesses. Similar to stockbrokers, the public will first seek intermediaries who have the reputation worthy of their trust. When an owner/ seller advertises one specific business for sale, most of the response will come from potential buyers who are presently interested only in the industry, trade, or profession advertised. This will be a very limited response. If potential buyers see a number of interesting business types and are additionally attracted to the perceived expertise of the intermediary, the same advertising dollars will bring a much larger response.

Since most buyers in the market never buy the type of business in which they originally have an interest, the intermediary offering many types of businesses will have a great advantage over a single seller offering only his/her business. Not only is the single seller at risk from a standpoint of confidentiality, he/she is more likely to find more potential buyers working through an intermediary offering several business types and maintaining the confidence of the public.

Appropriate steps exercised by the intermediary are of real value to sellers in maintaining confidentiality. A seller never needs to be concerned about any potential buyers until they have been preliminarily screened by the intermediary. It is not unusual for some large intermediary firms to have over 250 inquiries about a specific business before the seller actually meets the buyer who ultimately makes the purchase. The 249 potential buyers the seller did not meet represent hundreds of hours of time that could have frustrated the seller and ruined his/her business in the process.

STEPS TO CONSIDER IN MAINTAINING CONFIDENTIALITY

1. In all advertising and promotional materials, never reveal any of the following which may allow someone to guess the identity of the business:

    (a) Specific information about unusually limited numbers of businesses.

    (b) Specific name of the town in which business is located. Usually the state is enough and definitely not more than a specific region of the state.

    (c) Specific name of unusually limited numbers of products or services.

    (d) Information which would reveal owner(s) or primary service providers.

    (e) Outstanding awards unique to the business, owner, or employees.

2. Never allow potential buyers to have any identifying information on a business through the mail, fax, or electronically until they:

    (a) Properly identify themselves with the minimum of a state driver's license number.

    (b) Sign adequately written nondisclosure agreement.

    (c) Understand your proper agency relationship.

3. Never allow potential buyers to visit the business or meet owner(s) unless they are in the presence of the intermediary and until they:

    (a) Have shown themselves capable of financially handling the transaction.

    (b) Have shown themselves capable of managing the business or securing someone who can.

   (c)   Signed document(s) verifying agency relationship(s) of intermediary.

   (d)   Understand they are additionally responsible for all third party professionals to whom they share information about the business.

   (e)   Beyond (d.) above referenced, they may not share information with anyone.

   (f)   If they do not proceed with negotiations, they are to immediately return all information previously given to them.

4. Do not allow anyone else associated with potential buyers to have access to any information unless:

   (a)   Buyer with whom you are working has signed responsibility for their confidentiality.

   (b)   The new person or entity signs nondisclosure agreement for themselves.

5. Maintain all records of all parties for the length of time required by your state and/or profession.

6. Treat other professionals and cooperating intermediaries with the same confidentiality standards you use with potential buyers, no exceptions!

Confidentiality is the trademark of the intermediary and should be a concern of all professionals serving sellers and buyers. Obviously the seller has the greatest concern because he/she stands to lose the most if confidentiality is not maintained.

Steps to maintain confidentiality are shared in almost every chapter of this book because the concern touches every stage of buying and selling businesses. All professionals are entrusted with information which is not to be shared with anyone who is not a potential party to the transaction, and then only after they have signed a nondisclosure statement. Those who sign the statement and receive the information must be made aware of their responsibility to maintain confidentiality. In over 25 years of serving buyers and sellers I cannot remember a single time when the loss of confidentiality became a serious issue. Actually, it seems buyers and sellers are more guilty of carelessness in confidentiality than the professionals. Nevertheless, everyone involved must make it their number one concern.

CONFIDENTIALITY CANNOT BE GUARANTEED

Let's be realistic! Confidentiality cannot be guaranteed, so we must discuss options to be used when someone who is not a party to the transaction becomes aware or suspicious of the negotiations. Some of the following may be helpful responses for potential sellers:

1. It is important that legitimate parties to the privileged information not appear alarmed when approached about the possibility of a business being for sale. To show undue concern is to look suspicious. Always respond calmly as if it is the farthest thing from your mind.

2. Don't be afraid to admit that it could happen because everything is for sale at the right price. However, no person in their right mind would pay what it would take to buy this business. But be assured, when someone offers a million more than it's worth, it's sold.

3. In fact, there have been interested parties, but they always run when they hear the price. Isn't it nice to have what everyone else wants!

Buyers also have a concern for the confidentiality of their participation in business searches and negotiations. Not only do they have responsibility in handling the information of potential sellers, buyers do not want to appear anxious to buy a business. When approached about their interest or participation in negotiations of a particular business, they will want to respond calmly with statements such as:

1. Well, I guess I might be interested if it were for sale. Have you heard it was for sale? I seriously doubt they would sell that business.
2. Actually, I don't think it is worth my time. There is no way anyone in their right mind would take an offer as low as I would make.
3. I really have more than I can handle right now. How in the world could I look after another business?

The sharing of confidential information is a sign of gross immaturity! If one represents himself/herself as a professional, the first step is strict adherence to confidentiality, no exceptions. Be a good example and don't tolerate anything less in others.

10

OFFERS TO PURCHASE THAT RESULT IN CLOSINGS

(The Intermediary Is Normally the Coordinator of Paperwork and Activities of Other Professionals)

Laws regarding buying and selling businesses vary from state to state, which makes it necessary for all parties involved to secure adequate legal advice in each step of the process. As a general rule, intermediaries coordinate the flow of paperwork and other professionals involved, but are not allowed to prepare the documents unless they are promulgated by state agencies, prepared by attorneys for their use, or the intermediary is a party to the agreement.

Buyers and sellers often use the services of several professionals, but always depend on intermediaries to be responsible for everyone performing in a timely manner so all actions consummate in a successful closing. Each professional has his/her own expertise to add to the transaction to fulfill their fiduciary to the principal they represent with each one's participation and/or advice limited to his/her own specific field of training, licensing, and certification.

If both the buyer and seller did not intend to actually complete the transaction, there would not be an offer to purchase which clearly states they intend to do so. Since it is the goal of the buyer and seller to complete a successful closing, it should also be the goal of each professional involved. It is disappointing to all when one or more professionals allow their personal egos to distract or obstruct the progress. If the purchase is not financed by the seller, lenders will have an important role. It is important that language and conditions of the offer to purchase agreement be prepared in terms acceptable to standard lending practices. The intermediary has been involved from the beginning and is responsible for seeing the project through to the end. If anyone has not responded and/or completed their assigned task(s) within 72 hours, the intermediary should find the delaying hindering cause and initiate a correction.

THE BINDING OFFER TO PURCHASE AGREEMENT

Even though it may have been preceded by a letter of intent, at this point in negotiations there should be a binding offer to purchase signed by the potential buyer which is to be presented to the seller by the intermediary. This should be done almost immediately; however, it must first be clearly understood by the presenter. Since many documents involve several pages of verbiage, I have found it helpful in my own understanding to condense everything to an outline of no more than one page. This allows a visual understanding of the most important items in one glance. Each offer is different, but I often start my condensed outline with one similar to the example at the end of this chapter (Exhibit 10.1). It is important that the disclaimer be included at the bottom of the page if it is to be shown to the seller. This outline is mostly a brief explanation of the financial aspects and it is important to stress there are many other vital parts of the offer. The seller will want to respond in a timely manner to maintain the momentum of the negotiations!

COUNTEROFFER(S)

The presentation to the seller will often result in a counteroffer from the seller to the buyer. I am not comfortable with marking the changes on the original document. Instead, I like the use of a separate instrument which states the changes desired by the seller and is attached to the original document. Some negotiations will involve the use of several counters from both the seller and buyer. Consequently, it may be appropriate to start over with a fresh document if the counters become confusing. A copy of some of the items to be considered in a counteroffer are found at the end of the chapter (Exhibit 10.2). All of these negotiations and transfer of paperwork should be done in a timely manner. However, if the time allowed by either party is about to expire, an extension of offer to purchase will be needed. A copy of some ideas for this is included at the end of the chapter (Exhibit 10.3).

CONFIRMATION OF FEES AND DISCLAIMER(S)

When both buyer and seller finally agree on all terms and conditions and have signed the acceptable offer to purchase agreement, it is important that the intermediary have both sign his/her disclaimer. Additionally, the seller should confirm the fee due the intermediary in writing (Exhibit 10.4) and both instruments should be attached to the offer to purchase. Some professionals prefer to have this accomplished by the closing agent; however, my opinion is the sooner the better! Suggestions for this are included in Chapter 8.

CONTINGENCIES

The final agreement may contain contingencies which must be removed by the party(s) making them a condition of the offer to purchase agreement (Exhibit 10.5). The intermediary is the coordinator of this process and must be sure this is accomplished within the time allowed.

POTENTIAL NEGOTIATED CONCERNS
OF BUYERS AND SELLERS

Beginning intermediaries and first-time buyers and sellers often ask for some advance indication of negotiated items which they may face during the process. Space only allows a very limited number.

1. Subject to third-party financing.
2. Subject to buyer assuming portions of current financing.
3. Buyer's financial due-diligence of seller's records.
4. Seller to pay or be responsible for all nonassumed liabilities, including taxes prior to closing.
5. Buyer may want to hold back a portion of the down

payment in escrow for a predetermined period for protection against undisclosed liabilities.

6. Buyer may want to be able to offset future payments for a period of time after closing for protection against undisclosed liabilities.

7. Seller to indemnify buyer from all merchandise and/or service warranties prior to closing.

8. Seller to indemnify buyer against all claims of operations prior to closing.

9. Seller to provide a training/transition period.

10. Seller will covenant to not compete for a negotiated time and geographical area and/or a specific client or customer list.

11. All inventory to be usable and salable at closing.

12. All furniture, fixtures, equipment, and machinery in operating condition at closing.

13. Telephone numbers, and so on to remain with the business.

14. Name(s) of business to remain the same with dba (doing business as) given to buyer with no transfer of previous liability.

15. All parties to the contract will have the right to have all documents reviewed by attorneys of their choice.

16. Prorations to be confirmed.

17. Buyer may want seller to remain and sign an employment contract for a period of time.

18. If the offer to purchase is not exclusive to the buyer and seller receives another offer before closing, buyer may want a period of time to show evidence of funds and make the offer exclusive with earnest money at risk.

19. Seller may want offer to contain earnest money at risk with other significant penalties if buyer does not close within a certain time allowed.

20. Both buyer and seller may want investigative due-diligence provisions as well as financial due-diligence.

21. Seller and buyer to fully cooperate with all investigations.

22. Seller and buyer to pay for negotiated portions of inspections, due-diligence, and so on.

23. If real property is involved, all required forms to be completed by all parties.

24. Seller will not hire away current or future employees for a period of time.

25. Buyer will not use sensitive information to compete with seller if sale is not completed.

26. Buyer agrees not to assign contract or sell business until seller has been paid in full.

27. Buyer agrees to not encumber or relocate any assets until seller has been paid in full.

28. Buyer agrees to maintain negotiated level of inventory, furniture, fixtures, equipment, and machinery until seller has been paid in full.

29. Buyer will provide regular financial statements on a negotiated timetable until seller has been paid in full.

30. Seller has inspection rights until paid in full.

31. The physical address of the business will not be changed until seller has been paid in full.

32. Buyer's stockholders agree not to sell or in any way encumber their stock until seller has been paid in full.

Exhibit 10.1

Analysis of Offer

Date of offer: ___/___/___
Name of business: _____
Seller: _____
Buyer making offer: _____
Contingencies: _____
_____
_____

	1.	*Selling price*	$	_____
(-)	2.	Escrow deposit(s)		_____
(-)	3.	Cash at closing		_____
(+/-)	4.	Prorations		_____
(+/-)	5.	Inventory (over/under)		_____
(+/-)	6.	Other (over/under): _____		_____
(-)	7.	Notes:		
		a. Assumed: _____		_____
		b. Wrapped: _____		_____
		c. New (third party): _____		_____
		d. Other note(s): _____		_____
(-)	8.	Other: _____		_____
(=)	9.	*Balance due seller*		
		Paid as follows:		
		a. Note 1: _____		_____
		b. Note 2: _____		_____
		c. Other: _____		_____
		d. Other: _____		_____
	10.	*Total deferred due seller:*		
		(9a + 9b + 9c + 9d)		_____
	11.	*Total consideration due seller:*		
		(2 + 3 +/- 4 +/- 5 +/- 6 + 10)		_____
(-)	12.	Fee/commission due intermediary		_____
(-)	13.	Other professional fees: _____		_____
(-)	14.	Closing costs: _____		_____
(=)	15.	*Net consideration to seller*	$	_____

Note: This is only a preliminary estimate and does not necessarily represent all factors of the true value of the transaction to the seller or buyer. Please read the entire document.

Exhibit 10.2

Counteroffer

Parties:

Business:

I/we accept all of the terms and conditions of the offer to purchase and sale of assets agreement dated ____, except as follows:

Should the ___ buyer, ___ seller fail to accept this counteroffer on or before _____ o'clock ___ A.M., ___ P.M. on _____, 19___, this counteroffer is revoked and the deposit will be returned, in full, to buyer. The intermediary is authorized to deposit the earnest money deposit on behalf of the parties to this agreement with the escrow agent in a timely manner. Receipt of a copy of this counteroffer is hereby acknowledged by all parties.

Signatures:

| _____ | | _____ | |
| Seller | Date | Buyer | Date |

| _____ | | _____ | |
| Seller | Date | Buyer | Date |

Exhibit 10.3

Extension of Offer to Purchase

Extension #: _____

Business: _____

Address _____

Seller _____

Buyer _____

Whereas, buyer has made an offer to purchase the above referenced business; and whereas, said offer to purchase calls for a response from the seller by the following date:

_____

Now, therefore, it is agreed by the buyer that the response date shall be extended to the following date:

_____ at: _____ o'clock, _____ A.M. _____ P.M.

And that all other terms of the offer to purchase shall remain the same, until they are accepted, rejected, or countered by the seller within the time above referenced.

Executed this _____ day of _____, 19___.

Signatures:

_____
Buyer

_____
Seller

_____
Intermediary

Exhibit 10.4

Confirmation of Fee Agreement

The undersigned seller(s) and _____ (intermediary), hereby agree on the offer to purchase agreement dated: ___/___/___, on the business known as:

_____

Located at: _____

Seller(s): _____

Buyer(s): _____

Seller(s) and intermediary confirm that the previously signed sole and exclusive agreement, dated: ___/___/___, calls for the following fees to be paid to intermediary:

_____

Other considerations due intermediary:

_____

Seller(s) hereby agree and confirm that these fees and considerations are due intermediary:

_____

Seller(s) hereby instruct escrow/closing agent to pay the above referenced fees and considerations to intermediary from funds due seller.

Receipt of a copy of this agreement is hereby acknowledged by seller and intermediary.

Date: ___/___/___

_____   _____
Seller   Intermediary

_____   _____
Corporate officer if seller   Corporate officer if
is a corporation   intermediary is a
                              corporation

Exhibit 10.5

Contingency Removal

We, the undersigned buyers of that certain business known as:

_____

Located at: _____

do hereby remove the contingencies from that certain offer to purchase agreement dated:

_____

between buyer: _____

and seller: _____

The contingencies removed are:

_____

_____

_____

_____

_____

All other terms and conditions of the offer to purchase agreement remain unchanged and in full force and effect.

Date: __/__/__

Signatures:

_____

Buyer(s)

_____

Seller(s)

11

THE PROFESSIONAL TEAM APPROACH TO EFFECTIVE CLOSINGS

THE TEAM

The intermediary, who initially introduced the principals of the transaction and reconciled all of the activities that are now consummating in a transfer of ownership, is still the appropriate one to coordinate the events all the way through funding and exchange of documents at the closing table. In addition to the buyer, seller, and intermediary, others could be a part of this important team:

Accountant(s)

Attorney(s)

Tax specialist(s)

Estate planner(s)

Escrow/closing agent(s)

Appraiser(s)

Banker(s)

Others

The buyer and seller have agreed to close the transaction, which should be the same goal of all professionals involved, regardless of their temporary assignment of reaching the highest possible level of achievement in their respective fields. It is the responsibility of the intermediary to become a reconciliation expert as he/she keeps the process on course toward everyone's ultimate goal of the closing.

COACHING THE TEAM

From the beginning, each party to the transaction must feel and act as part of the team. Every team needs an effective coach who sets an example of unselfish cooperation.

Coordination of the individual events seems to often fall into these categories:

1. All parties must agree on the final set of instructions which are assembled and delivered to the escrow/closing agent by the intermediary. Every transaction has its own unique ingredients, but the general form provided at the end of this chapter (Exhibit 11.1) will be helpful in putting together all information needed by the escrow/closing agent. The principals should understand these instructions and initial the bottom of each page before they are given to the escrow/closing agent.

2. In some instances the escrow/closing agent will be a licensed attorney who will also prepare the documents to

be used at closing. This person must view himself/herself as a dealmaker who will often provide assistance regarding the structuring of the transaction from a legal perspective.

These services, which can cover both asset and stock purchases, include the preparation of closing documents, comprised of the settlement sheets, bill of sale, promissory note, security agreement, financing statement, trade name filings, noncompetition agreement, corporate resolutions, real property and equipment lease assignments, and any other relevant documents. The services may also include a Uniform Commercial Code (UCC) lien search, personal property tax prorations, and verifying corporate standing. Other escrow services include the post-closing escrow of funds and/or documents. Fees for these services should be chargeable to the principal parties to the acquisition and not to the intermediary.

Some of these legal firms have also prepared a form asset purchase agreement which is available for use in the sale and purchase of businesses. This type of agreement should be commonly used in business acquisitions and should provide an additional advantage of avoiding potential claims against the intermediary regarding the drafting of legal documents. It is important to research the legal ramifications of all these procedures in the state in which you provide your services as a professional. If this is not the case, the intermediary must additionally act as a prompter to keep the timing of this and other elements on track.

3. Solving the unexpected problems on a timely basis and the establishment of a harmonious understanding during disagreements will ultimately confirm the need for the intermediary. Don't delay, start each day with your first

activities directed at getting updated on all scheduled closings.

4. The closing is often held at the office of the escrow/closing agent with the intermediary unobtrusively coaching the team across the goal line. In some states, the intermediary is held responsible for the accuracy of the closing, even though other professionals may contribute important parts. Whether an intermediary is legally responsible or not, he/she must act responsibly.

5. The funding may take place at the closing table or it may happen later, depending upon the requirements of the financial arrangements, and so on. Regardless, the intermediary will remain a helper until the end.

SUCCESSFUL TEAMS PLAY TO THE END OF THE GAME

Even though proper filings may be the responsibility of other professionals, it is a good idea for the intermediary to leave friendly reminders of these responsibilities. Each business opportunity transaction is a commercial transaction. In every state in the union, commercial transactions are governed by the Uniform Commercial Code (UCC). UCC articles relevant to business closings include sales, commercial paper, bulk transfers (in certain states), secured transactions, fraudulent transfers, and fraud.

Since seller financing is an option often used in business sales, all parties to the transaction are well advised to be familiar with the provisions in UCC Article 3, relative to commercial paper. In essence, commercial paper includes drafts, checks, certificates of deposit, and promissory notes.

Article 3 governs the liability of the parties with respect to promissory notes and rights and duties of the parties to the note. Article 3 also governs the guaranty of promissory notes.

A closely related segment is Article 9, which deals with secured transactions. A note is usually secured by a security agreement which is perfected by a financing statement. This article deals with the taking and *perfecting* of a security interest and the related rights, duties, and liabilities of the parties. Article 9 describes when filing is required to perfect a security interest, what types of filings are necessary, and when possession of collateral is necessary for the perfection of a security interest.

Since rules in the states vary regarding the place and procedures for UCC filings, local compliance is essential. Article 6 (in states where it has not been repealed) deals with bulk sales transactions and basically requires that creditors of a seller must be notified prior to the closing or those creditors can assert their claim against the buyer for a period of time after the closing. As an added item, the buyer and seller will appreciate a reminder regarding their responsibility to the IRS in the filing of Form 8594, the asset acquisition statement, which must be attached to their federal income tax statement.

Exhibit 11.1

Information Provided to Escrow/Closing Agent

1. *Information regarding seller:*

   FEI#:   S.S. #:

   State Sales Tax #:

   Franchise Tax #:

   Other Tax Information:

   Structure:

   _____ Corporation, type: _____

   If Corporation, name officers, shareholders, and directors:

   _____ Partnership, type: _____

   If Partnership, name partners:

   _____ LLC, type: _____

   If LLC, name managers and members:

   _____ Sole Proprietorship, Social Security #:_____

   Address:

   City: State: Zip:

   County: Other jurisdiction(s):

   Telephones:

   Name and address to use for notice purposes:

   If Corporation, give Charter Number, if available:

   ____ Secure Certificate of Good Standing from the local office of the State Comptroller or Secretary of State?

   ____ Provide Resolution/authorization.

2. *Information regarding buyer:*

FEI #:   S.S. #:

State Sales Tax #:

Franchise Tax #:

_____ Corporation, type: _____

If Corporation, name officers, shareholders, and directors:

_____ Partnership, type: _____

If Partnership, name officers:

_____ LLC, type: _____

If LLC, name managers and members:

_____Sole Proprietorship, Social Security #: _____

Address:

City: State: Zip:

County: Other jurisdiction(s):

Telephones:

Name and address to use for notice purposes:

If Corporation, give Charter #: ____

____ Secure Certificate of Good Standing from local office of the State Comptroller or Secretary of State?

____ Provide Resolution/Authorization.

3. *Potential documents for asset sale to be prepared by attorney:*

____ Asset purchase agreement
____ Bill of sale
____ Promissory note(s)

(continued)

279

Exhibit 11.1 (continued)

____ Promissory note assumption agreement(s)
____ Security agreement
____ Financing statement
____ Affidavit/indemnity of debts/liens
____ Disclaimer(s)
____ Disbursement of funds at closing
____ Prorations
____ Settlement statements
____ Corporation resolution(s) or partnership
      authorization(s)
____ Corporate certificate(s) of good standing
____ Articles of amendment
____ Withdrawal of trade name(s)
____ Certificate of trade name(s)
____ File UCC financing statement(s)
____ UCC lien searches
____ Release of landlord lien(s)
____ Release of tax lien(s)
____ Equipment lease assignment(s)
____ Bulk sales act requirements
____ Contingency release statement(s)
____ Real property lease(s)
____ Noncompetition agreement(s)
____ IRS Form 8594
____ Other:

4. *Potential real estate documents to be prepared by attorney:*

____ Purchase agreement
____ Warranty deed
____ Promissory note(s)
____ Deed of trust or mortgage
____ All-inclusive note and deed of trust
____ Assumption
____ Deed of trust
____ Title commitment and title policy
____ Closing statement
____ Prorations
____ Disbursement of funds

5. *Real estate information provided:*

Physical address:

Legal description:

Survey to be provided:

    Provided by: Paid by:

Property plat provided:

Description of buildings and improvements:

Copies of liens:

Tax receipts:

Title policy:

    Provided by: Paid by:

Zoning/use restrictions attached:

Status of mineral rights:

Status of surface/air rights:

Status of easements/encroachments:

Other:

6. *Financial information:*

Allocation of price:

    Real estate (land):

        (Bldg.):

    Furniture/fixtures/equipment/machinery:

    Inventory:

    Consulting/employment agreement(s):

    Noncompetition agreement(s):

    Other:

    Total:

(continued)

Exhibit 11.1 (continued)

Total escrow received:

Escrow deposited in:

Person responsible for escrow:

Terms of purchase:

    All cash: ____ Yes ____ No

    Pay out:

        Amount paid at closing:

        Note 1:

            Terms:

        Note 2:

            Terms:

        Note 3:

            Terms:

        Other:

7. *Assets purchased:*

    Counted/verified by: _____ Date: _____

8. *Assets not included in sale:*

9. *Liabilities assumed by purchaser:*

10. *Inventory purchased:*

    Counted/verified by: _____ Date: _____

11. *Earnest money offer to purchase agreement signed on:*
    __/__/__

    Copy attached: ____ Yes ____ No

12. *Commissions/professional fees due:*

    $_____ to: _____

    $_____ to: _____

    $_____ to: _____

    $_____ to: _____

13. *Noncompetition agreement:* ____ years for area: _____

    Compensation of \$_____ to: _____

    Payments: _____

14. *Employment/consultant agreement:* ____ years

    Compensation of \$_____ to: _____

    Payments: _____

15. *Training/transition period of:* _____

    Provided to:_____

    Provided by:_____

16. *Items handled outside of escrow:*

17. *Trade name(s):*

    Date(s) filed:

    Where filed:

18. *Miscellaneous:*

    List of F/F/E&M attached: ____ Yes ____ No

    List of seller's creditors attached: ____ Yes ____ No

    Insurance provided: ____ Yes ____ No

    Occupancy permit provided: ____ Yes ____ No

    Any deposits transferred: ____ Yes ____ No, which ones:

    Name to be used by buyer for business:

    Time/date buyer will take possession: ___/___/___

    Buyer notified to bring certified funds to closing: ____ Yes ____ No

    Copy of canceled checks for taxes attached: ____ Yes ____ No

    Sales tax receipts attached: ____ Yes ____ No

(continued)

Exhibit 11.1 (continued)

Certificate of good standing secured/attached: ____ Yes ____ No

Sole and exclusive right to sell agreement attached: ____ Yes ____ No

Verification of commissions/fees due attached: ____ Yes ____ No

Existing leases attached: ____ Yes ____ No

Closing date/time:

Closing location:

Parties due at closing:

Signatures:

_____
Seller(s)   Date

_____
Buyer(s)   Date

_____
Intermediary   Date

_____
Received by escrow/closing agent   Date

12

TRAITS THAT CREATE FOCUSED INTERMEDIARIES

I was recently asked to speak at a combined conference of three associations of professionals involved in valuing, buying, and selling businesses. The topic assigned to me was "Organizing the M&A Practice . . . How to Do the Right Things First." A similar topic was given to me for a speaking assignment at another national conference in our industry with their choice of subject being "Professional Priority Planning." In both instances, those responsible for program planning explained the need for practical solutions in making daily priority decisions to produce better results for clients and increased income for professionals.

This is obviously not a unique problem in our industry. All professionals wrestle with the calendar and the most profitable use of time, talents, and resources. A major university study revealed *50% of all professionals never survive* the initial learning curve which can take up to two years. Even more distressing was *90% never experience real success* in a sales or professional service career because they cannot deal with the ups and downs of income streams in a commission or fee structured environment. The most alarming statistic in the study was *99% never retire with complete financial security* because they ignore the reality of ultimate financial responsibility. After over 25 years of training and motivating people in our business, I really don't think our numbers are any better than other professions. Individuals and companies in the United States collectively spend millions of dollars trying to meet these needs with training which too often becomes temporary feeble shots of motivational adrenaline. Why? Could the answer be we have collected too many answers, when in reality, there seems to be only a few that really work for those who are part of the *1% who really win big in life*!

Those who depend on commissions, professional fees, and/or own their own businesses must learn to deal with the roller coaster more commonly known as the inconsistency of their gross income and net cash flow. Roller coasters are also the ups and downs of temporary thrills of accomplishment followed by frustrating disappointments. Wouldn't you like to stop this hectic existence for life and find things you can trust to smooth out these hills and valleys? Aren't we all looking for something to be excited about following the rest of our careers? In reality, life is a daily climb. It can be much more rewarding if we can trust something to make the end of that climb become the top of our mountain. I want to encourage you to continue your aggressive search until you find a blueprint for life which will reduce these temporary frustrations and produce the *ultimate goal of true financial security and personal happiness.*

Do you need help? I'm told by some of those in the top 1% the fact of their achievement is all the motivation they need to continue taking advantage of every opportunity to improve. They did not achieve their success by accident and they will do anything necessary to improve their focus to stay there. They need help more than anyone because it's more difficult to stay in the 1% than end up in the 99%. What about those in the 99% who feel they cannot afford the time or expense to improve their focus? Actually, this may be a sign they are in emergency need of help! Until you find what works for you, you cannot afford not to keep looking . . . you must find it to survive. We all need a more defined focus and refined skills. Our career can become like a spaceship off course. The longer we wait to correct it, the more we will spin out of control.

As we search for the secret, the greatest achievers are our cheerleaders:

"Most people are about as successful as they make up their minds to be."

—Abraham Lincoln

For simplicity, I've organized this effort into a three-step process:

Step 1.   Survival
Step 2.   Success
Step 3.   Security

Happiness and success are your birthright, but not guaranteed. You must get in harmony with the requirements that guarantee them. You must keep all three steps in focus on a daily basis! There is a common thread running through all steps. Without all three, you have no fabric.

Step 1   Survival

"To live is to suffer, to Survive is to find meaning in the suffering."

—*Viktor Frankl*

You would think the next to the oldest profession in the world (sales) would have found the secrets by now. They've been known for generations but only 1% are willing to narrow their focus enough to follow them. Here's your chance, but you have to take full responsibility to do it on your own. This is not a roller coaster ride. This is a train on track that leads straight to your wildest dreams. You are the conductor, fireman, ticket taker, passenger, and benefactor! Here is the track, or at least one of them. Get on, fasten your seat belts and get going!

Survival means developing skills to match any economy. All economies are dangerous, even the so-called good ones which afford the opportunity to start bad habits. These good times are often when we ignore the necessity of staying focused. And, then come the bad ones when the temporary struggles fool you into thinking there is no immediate hope and you fall into the trap of waiting for the next good economy. Does this sound like a roller coaster to you?

If you are not willing to make the following pledges, you may as well sell your train and get off the track so others can pass.

I WILL BALANCE ALL BUDGETS UNDER MY RESPONSIBILITY!

Put yourself in a financial fail-safe position by immediately creating budgets that can be balanced. Cut expenses, reduce debt, and face reality. Don't make any commitments for any additional expenditures until all budgets allow you to save a minimum of 10% of all net cash flow. Make a list of everything owned by every entity for which you are responsible and consider the value of retaining each of them.

> "To be without some of the things you want is an indispensable part of (survival and) happiness."
> —*Bertrand Russell*

I WILL SPEND MY TIME, EFFORTS, AND RESOURCES DOING WHAT I DO (AND LOVE) BEST

This industry involves selling. You either sell a business or a service (valuation) and most of all you sell yourself. The best investment you can ever make is to buy 100 shares of yourself! Set aside a specific amount or percentage of earnings to improve yourself through professional education in sales, salesmanship, time management, or specific techniques in your industry. You can attend conventions, conferences, and seminars. You can also turn your automobile into a classroom by buying sales, motivational, or educational tapes. Listen to them more than once so the techniques become ingrained in you and it all becomes second nature. A few dollars spent in improving yourself will yield thousands in additional commissions and fees. Be honest about your profession and your love for it. Love may not be a term with which you are comfortable, but you must come to terms with whatever best represents your deepest motivations which cause you to give your personal best.

If you are not comfortable with the requirements of selling, it's time for a reality check. Stop right here and write your *mission statement* and then live up to it daily.

> "Choose a job you love, and you will never have to work a day in your life."
>
> —*Confucius*

I WILL BECOME COMFORTABLE WITH THE REQUIREMENT OF SACRIFICE

I cannot be true to the honesty requirements of this exercise without stressing that sacrifice is an important step that normally precedes most great accomplishments. Anything worth achieving is usually not found at the end of a smooth road. The immigrants who came, and are still coming, to the United States are wonderful examples. I recently saw four families of immigrants willing to sacrifice and live together in one small house in order to achieve the American dream. There is a difference in sacrifice and unnecessary suffering. If the cause is avoidable don't waste yourself on it. If not, make the necessary sacrifices based on attainable goals.

> "He who has a why . . ., can bear with almost any how."
>
> —*Viktor Frankl*

Step 2   Success

FORCED-FOCUS, THE AUTOPILOT FOR SUCCESS

Humans are different from most everything else on the planet regarding their ability to stay focused for extended periods of time. You can put an airplane on autopilot and it will stay there. Put a fish in the water and it has no desire to lay on the beach in the sun. Put an eagle in the air and it does not want to swim in the sea. Put a seed in the ground and its tendency is to grow straight up. Give the average human something to do and they will lose their focus on a regular basis. What is it that causes humans this great difficulty? Maybe it's our desire for experimentation and change, both of which are excellent traits if exercised properly.

What can we do to help people reach a reasonable balance between their desire for experimentation and the required ability to stay focused on ultimate goals?

First, we must determine the ultimate objective, and if it has anything to do with money or personal success, we have to take the thought process to the final stage. For most of the 1% that means *ultimate personal financial freedom*, which comes through enough income from interest on unencumbered investments to exceed expenses for the rest of their lives. This frees them to finally spend their time doing whatever means the most to them, whenever they want to do it.

Second, realize educational, mental, and emotional adjustments are not enough to make it happen. We cannot stay focused with these efforts alone. We need something more dependable and unchangeable to keep us from diverting our energies and resources.

Third, understand that nothing is a permanent motivation. Until I find the perfect one, I'm sure impressed with what I think is the current best. I'm not referring to some great mystery which can only be obtained by the privileged few. It can be understood and utilized in any discipline of life, especially the valuing, buying, and selling of businesses.

Physical reminders are the ultimate tool to stay focused on the task before us at all times, especially when the adrenaline of motivational training has slipped away. Most married couples wear wedding bands to remind themselves (and others) of their total commitment. Engineers place road signs and even concrete barriers on the highways to keep drivers focused because the world cannot deal with each of us redesigning the roads as we travel. This is what I call *forced-focus*. Physical reminders are effective because they are like tattoos. They are obvious, they don't go away, they don't have moods, and they don't lose their enthusiasm and motivation. They just stay there and keep reminding you. I'm not trying to take away your freedom of choice. You make your own ultimate goals and set your own physical reminders and you even have the freedom to not participate. After all, somebody has to help make up the 99%. Specific physical reminders will be mentioned as we proceed. If you don't like the ones suggested, maybe you'll be motivated to think of your own.

TIME MANAGEMENT PRINCIPLES THAT CREATE MORE BUSINESS

Everyone uses some form of daily, weekly, monthly, and yearly planners for structure (*Physical reminder #1*). Owning a calendar/organizer is not the problem. The problem is that most of them were designed by someone who knows nothing about our industry. How much time you spend is important, but not as important as what you do during this time. If your planner does not focus your time in the right activities, it simply becomes a written record of where you should not have spent your time. A planner must force you to spend your time on the right priorities. First, I'll share with you some of the principles that should be a part of your planner and then I'll give you some organizational structure to *force-focus* your planner.

Billable hours are those for which we get paid because we are engaged in specific tasks and are *paid by the hour*. Some professionals who charge flat fees, up-front fees, commissions, and who own their own businesses are often proud they are not forced to punch a clock or justify how they spend their time. The enjoyment of this freedom will often cause you to not actually use all of your time in financially gainful activities. This carelessness will cause you to lose income *by the hour* which can never be reclaimed. The challenge is to be diligent in the use of each hour as if we were required to justify it.

Physical reminder #2 is a dramatic exercise to help you determine if you are spending your hours in financially gainful activities. Buy a stopwatch and wear it 24 hours a day for six weeks. Turn it on when you are engaged in activities that directly affect your income and turn it off the second you are doing things for which you will not be paid. At the end of each day and week, compare the net hours registered on your stopwatch with the hours you thought you worked. I hope you are ready for this potential shock!

Here's another lesson from my Dad, a very successful professional who did not work for someone else *by the hour*. *Physical reminder #3* is my Dad's buckeye bean, which grows on a bush in east Texas and reaches the size and look of the eye of a deer, hence the name buckeye bean. He regularly examined his income which was divided by the number of new persons he needed to contact on a daily basis to keep an adequate flow of new business. Each morning he would renew his commitment to contact this specific number of new prospects as he put the buckeye bean in his right pocket. He would keep an honest count of these new contacts during the day and would move the bean to his left pocket only when his goal was accomplished. He would not go home until the bean was in the left pocket. As a result of this commitment to a physical reminder, he spent the last years of his life fishing and hunting.

THE IMPORTANCE OF PRIORITY MANAGEMENT

Physical reminder #4 is a $50,000 lesson: *Being busy* is not necessarily *being profitable*. A major U. S. corporation was experiencing sales growth and at the same time becoming less profitable. The president assembled the finest experts who reported very loyal employees, many working overtime. In fact, this was the problem, everyone was doing too many things, most of which had nothing to do with profitability. Beginning with the president, the company needed a lesson in chasing the *closest, biggest dollar*. They immediately started the president using the physical reminder commonly known as the *top 10 things to do today*, the difference being they trained him to put the 10 things in the proper priority, as follows:

1. End each day making a list of everything needed to be accomplished the following day. Make the list a manageable number of 5, to no more than 10 items, not 25 to 30!
2. Rewrite the list, placing the items which would bring the most net profit the quickest, in sequence beginning at the top of the list.

3. If more than one item would bring net profit near the same time, place ones that would bring larger profits ahead of the others.

4. Then write the final list, placing priority on profits all the way down the list.

5. After finishing the list, place it on top of your desk and go home with the assurance of the next day being properly planned.

6. The next day, start at the top of the list and don't even read the second item until you have done all you can do on the first one. Why worry about the rest, they are less important!

The end of the year brought an exciting stockholders meeting at which was reported the largest profits in the history of the company. A $50,000 check was presented to the experts who originated the idea with the president.

Let's relate this physical reminder to our industry by creating a potential priority list of daily activities that *force-focus* us in earning the largest, closest fees. This might be the way an intermediary's daily planner should look:

1. Accomplish everything possible today on all closings scheduled.

2. Accomplish everything possible today on all transactions under contract.

3. Accomplish everything possible today on all activities that need to go to contract.

4. Schedule meetings between possible buyers and sellers.

5. Interview buyers . . . don't forget to suggest the need for valuations!

6. Make buyer appointments.

7. Call new buyer prospects.

8. Interview potential sellers . . . don't forget to suggest the need for valuations!

9. Make appointments with potential sellers.

10. Call new seller prospects.

11. Paperwork and other miscellaneous activities.

If the major portion of your income does not come from intermediary activities, use the same principles and make your own list of priorities that *force-focus* you to earn the closest, largest fees.

MORE PROSPECTS THAN YOU CAN HANDLE . . . JUST ASK FOR THEM!

On an airplane from Washington, DC to Houston, Texas, I sat by a lady who reminded me of a lesson previously learned, but forgotten because I had not tied it to a physical reminder. During the flight she convinced me to change my long distance service to her company. She could have sold me anything she wanted. In fact, I'm now married to her. After signing the agreement, she said: "My company requires me to secure three references from you. Would you please write their names and telephone numbers on the back of the agreement." Upon arriving in Houston, I called all three persons and told them to give me a good reference. In a few days each of them had called me back to say they received a call from her and had also signed with her company. Actually, she did not need the references, she wanted the prospects. This was her only marketing tool and it produced more prospects than she could handle. The lesson is to ask for three *referrals* from everyone with whom you talk about your industry, not just one or two. The math works better for you by threes!

CONQUER PROCRASTINATION, A BEAST WORSE THAN PORCUPINES

Volumes have been written about procrastination, most of which are better than anything I could share with you in a single paragraph. It is important to note that those who reach the top 1% conquer this beast and so should you! If your procrastination is the result of the fear of rejection, you must realize that no's are not always final and may only be a request for more information and a better selling job on your part. If you have a fear of failure, understand failure can be turned into a pause for reorganization, better attitudes, habits, and improvement. Conquer procrastination before it becomes a defeating habit. Don't procrastinate over the difficult and unpleasant. These tasks usually have larger rewards when accomplished and more damaging results when avoided.

Step 3   Security

I have always had goals, but too often they were just wish lists which faded away in the midst of temporary frustrations. This has been especially true with long-term goals. It is easier to stay focused on immediate, short-term, and intermediate goals. The desire for security is needed in all goal stages and especially required in long-term goals. My definition of security involves the financial ability to ultimately make my own decisions regarding the use of my time, energy, and resources. I realize the need for sacrifice along the way, but the final reward must make everything worthwhile in order to stay motivated.

Middle age has some significant benefits, and one of them is to realize that happiness does not necessarily come from having everything. Security comes from having enough to be personally responsible for yourself and others who depend upon you. Happiness comes from a healthy balance between health, financial, family, community, and spiritual responsibility. Maturity is a result of being capable of dealing with whichever of the above might be absent at any given time. Your definitions may be different and that's one of the wonderful advantages of achieving security.

The important thing is what you can do today in the ultimate achievement of security. Even though we are to enjoy the trip just as much as the destination when reached, it's the destination that initiates the decision to make the trip and keeps us in focus along the way. The love for the destination turns our goals into passions, not just wishes.

The important steps of *survival, success, and security* are all part of the whole and must be woven together with the love of what we do and those for whom we do it. Each step then becomes its own reward to be enjoyed along the way, as well as the ultimate goal!

Bottom Line:

1. Immediately take measures to guarantee your survival.
2. *Force-focus* your daily activities with priority planning specifically designed for success in your unique career choice.
3. Plan now for the date and type of security which will be an adequate reward for your efforts.

13

POTENTIAL CERTIFICATIONS AND LICENSING FOR INTERMEDIARIES

As previously indicated in the disclaimer by the author at the beginning of this book, every professional entering the industry must take personal responsibility for compliance with rules, regulations, and laws governing their activities. Since these liabilities vary from state to state it is not practical to make an effort at a specific listing of all potential requirements across the nation. The following general statements will provide the reader with common areas in which specific investigations should be made to determine possible requirements in each local, state, and national jurisdiction.

POTENTIAL CERTIFICATIONS

For these purposes, potential certifications are almost always optional to the professional and usually provided by a nonprofit trade association, organized for the purpose of offering education and certifications in business valuations and sales transactions. Each individual should check with the ones listed nationally to additionally locate others at state levels.

1. National associations offering education and certifications in Business Valuations:

   American Society of Appraisers
   P. O. Box 17265
   Washington, DC 20041
   Telephone: 800-ASA-VALU
   Certification offered: ASA

   American Institute of CPAs
   1211 Avenue of the Americas
   New York, NY 10036
   Telephone: 212-575-6200
   Certification offered: ABV (accredited in business valuation)

   Institute of Business Appraisers
   2240 W. Woolbright Rd. #407
   Boynton Beach, FL 33426
   Telephone: 561-732-3202
   Fax: 561-732-4304
   Email: IBAHQ@aol.com
   Contact Person: Tana Ewing
   Certification offered: CBA

2. National associations offering education and certification in business sales:

   International Business Brokers Association
   11250 Roger Bacon Drive, Suite 8
   Reston, VA 20190
   Telephone: 703-437-4377

Fax: 703-435-4390

Email: IBBAINC@aol.com

Contact Person: Administrator

Certification offered: CBI (certified business intermediary)

Institute of Certified Business Counselors

P. O. Box 70326

Eugene, OR 97401

Telephone: 541-345-8064

Fax: 541-726-2402

Contact Person: Wally Stabbert, President

Certification offered: CBC (Certified Business Counselor)

ABC Alliance of Business Consultants

(Membership offered exclusively to Business Consultants)

P. O. Box 460880

Aurora, CO 80046

Telephone: 303-627-0685

Fax: 303-627-0684

Contact Person: Bill Bumstead

Certification offered: PBC (Professional Business Consultant)

3. State Associations offering education and certification in business sales:

(Please see Industry Resource Section in back of book.)

POTENTIAL LICENSING AND REGISTRATION

1. Potential national licensing and registration requirements:

Securities and Exchange Commission

(Securities Exchange Act 1934)

450 5th Street NW

Washington, DC 20549

Telephone: 800-732-0330

Fax: 202-942-4194

Email: www.sec.gov

Contact Person: Division of Market Regulations, 202-942-0073

License offered: NASD Series 7, with others possibly appropriate.

NASD (National Association of Securities Dealers)

1735 K Street NW

Washington, DC 20006

Telephone: 202-728-8000

Email: www.NASDQ.com

Licenses offered: 30+/– different licenses available

Federal Trade Commission

(Disclosure Requirements & Prohibitions Concerning Franchising & Business Opportunity Ventures: 16 CFR Part 436)

600 Pennsylvania Avenue NW

Washington, DC 20580

Telephone: 202-326-3220

Fax: 202-326-3395

Contact Person: Steve Toporoff, 202-326-3135

Registration offered: Disclosure requirements and prohibitions should be explored.

2. Potential state licensing and registration requirements:

Since it is impractical to list all requirements for all states, for this exercise, we list only those for the state of Texas as examples. Interpretation of these rules and regulations is not guaranteed. Contact the specific state in which you will offer services for similar requirements:

Texas Real Estate Commission
(Texas Real Estate Act)
P. O. Box 12188
Austin, TX 78711-2188
Telephone: 512-465-3900
Fax: 512-465-3998
Email: www.TREC.STATE.TX.US
Contact Person: 800-250-8732
License(s) offered: real estate salesperson, real estate broker
Any salesperson involved in the sale of real estate (including leases) and/or indivisible contracts including real estate and non-real estate assets must have a Texas real estate sales or brokers license.

Texas State Securities Board
(The Securities Act, August 22, 1957, amended September 1, 1991)
P. O. Box 13167
Austin, TX 78711
Telephone: 512-305-8310
Fax: 512-305-8310
Email: www.SSB.STATE.TX.US
Contact Person: Dealer Division
License/Registration offered: For salespersons involved in the sale of a business through the transfer of stock of the corporation, from a *seller/operator* to a *buyer/operator* it appears there is a requirement for registration as a *securities dealer*, which provides for limited activities for participation in a stock sale.

Texas Appraiser Licensing and Certification Board
(HB-270, TALCB, 1991)
P. O. Box 12188
Austin, TX 78711-2188

Telephone: 512-465-3950
Fax: 512-465-3953
Email: TALBC@capnet.STATE.TX.US
License offered: Persons doing appraisals for federal related projects are required to have licenses for real property, but not for other assets.

Secretary of State, Business Opportunities Unit
(Tex. Rev. C.V. Stat. Ann Art. 5069-16.01 et Seq. Vernon 1987, Supp. '92)
P. O. Box 12887
Austin, TX 78711
Telephone: 512-475-1769
Fax: 512-475-2815
Email: AGARZA@www.sos.STATE.TX.US
Contact Person: Dorothy Wilson
Registration required: Salespersons names must be included in Schedule D of the registration requirements of the seller of the start-up business opportunity and/or franchisor, and this list must be updated every six months.

THE UNAUTHORIZED PRACTICE OF LAW (UPL)

Common misunderstandings exist all across the nation regarding the legal authority of intermediaries and other professionals in business sales in preparing documents. The crossroad appears in the use and preparation of so-called *standard forms* such as earnest money contracts and financing instruments to close a sale. Each state varies in the definition and enforcement of *unauthorized practice of law* (UPL) activities. The intermediary is advised to research applicable state laws and enforcement agencies. One state may have local bar associations investigate and prosecute, while others have committees directly attached to their highest courts. New Mexico has no UPL laws, California has a loose approach, and states like Texas and Florida engage in draconian enforcement. Recently, the supreme court of Texas obtained a permanent injunction against a real estate and securities licensed business broker. The injunction banned all use of legal forms, except those specifically approved by the statutory legal form section of the real estate board for use only by licensed brokers in real estate transactions.

In this chapter, the practice of law means the preparation of a pleading or other document incident to an action or special proceeding or the management of the action or proceeding on behalf of a client before a judge in court as well as a service rendered out of court, including the giving of legal advice or the rendering of any service requiring the use of legal skill or knowledge, such as preparing a will, contract, or other instrument, the legal effect of which under the facts and conclusions involved must be carefully determined. Texas Government Code, 81.101 (a).

Information in the section on UPL is provided by:

Jeffrey A. Lehmann, Attorney
Chairperson, District 4, The Unauthorized
    Practice of Law Committee
For the Supreme Court of Texas

GLOSSARY

Accounts Payable: A liability (debt) representing an amount owed to a creditor, usually arising from the purchase of merchandise or supplies; not necessarily due or past due.

Accounts Receivable: A claim against a debtor usually arising from sales or services rendered to the debtor; not necessarily due or past due.

Accrual Method: An accounting method of reporting in which expenses incurred and income earned for a given period are reported, although such expenses and income may not yet have actually been paid or received in cash, but have become fixed and definite.

Agency: A legal relationship resulting from an agreement or contract, either expressed or implied, written or oral, whereby one person, called the agent, is employed by another, called the principal, to do certain acts in dealing with a third party.

Agent: Any person, partnership, association, or corporation authorized or employed by another, called the principal, to act for, on behalf of, and subject to the control of the latter.

Amortization: (1) Liquidation or gradual retirement of a financial obligation by periodic installments. (2) Similar to the process by which tangible fixed assets are depreciated, the cost of intangible fixed assets possessing a determinable life should be systematically charged against revenue during each fiscal period by a process referred to as amortization. Unlike tangible fixed assets, where the accumulated depreciation to date is shown as a contra item subtracted from the original cost of the assets, intangible fixed assets are usually directly reduced by each period's amortization.

Appraisal: The act or process of determining value. It is synonymous with valuation as long as the same process is used.

Asset Sale: The sale of a business through transfer of ownership of tangible and/or intangible assets.

Backup Offer: An offer submitted to a seller with the understanding that the seller has already accepted a prior offer.

Balance Sheet: A statement showing a company's financial position at the end of an accounting period by listing an entity's assets, liabilities, and owner's equity.

Basis: The financial interest which the IRS attributes to the owner of an asset for purposes of determining annual depreciation and gain or loss on the sale of the asset. All property has a basis. If property was acquired by purchase, the owner's basis is the cost of the property plus the value of any capital expenditures for improvements, minus any depreciation actually taken or allowable. This new basis is called the property's Adjusted Basis.

Bill of Sale: A written agreement by which one person sells, assigns, or transfers his or her right to, or interest in, personal property to another.

Book Value: (1) With respect to assets, the capitalized cost of an asset less accumulated depreciation, depletion, or amortization as it appears on the books of account of the enterprise. (2) With respect to a business enterprise, the difference between total assets (net of depreciation, depletion, and amortization) and total liabilities of an enterprise as they appear on the balance sheet. It is synonymous with net book value, net worth, and shareholders' equity.

Bulk Transfer: Any transfer in bulk (and not a transfer in the ordinary course of the seller's business) of a major part of the materials, inventory, or supplies of an enterprise. The Uniform Commercial Code (UCC) regulates bulk transfers to deal with such commercial frauds as a merchant selling out his stock, pocketing the proceeds, and leaving his creditors unpaid.

Business Appraiser: A person who by education, training, and experience is qualified to make an appraisal of a business enterprise and/or its intangible assets.

Business Broker: See *Intermediary.*

Business Valuation: The act or process of arriving at an opinion or determination of the value of a business enterprise or an interest therein.

Buy-Sell Agreement: An agreement among partners or shareholders to the effect that one party will sell and another party will buy a business interest at a stated price upon the occurrence of a stated event, such as death, and so on.

Capital: The money and/or property comprising the wealth owned or used by a person or business enterprise; the accumulated wealth of a person or business.

Cash Basis: A method of recognizing revenues and expense when cash is received or disbursed rather than when earned or incurred.

Closing: The consummation of a transaction when the seller delivers title to the buyer in exchange for the purchase price.

Contingency: A provision placed in a contract which requires the completion of a certain act or the happening of a particular event before that contract becomes binding.

Contract: An agreement, enforceable at law, between two or more competent persons, having for its object a legal purpose, wherein the parties agree to act in a certain manner.

Corporation: An artificial person or legal entity created under state law, consisting of an association of individuals but regarded in law as having an existence and personality separate from such individuals. A corporation may be for profit or not for profit. The general powers of a corporation are enumerated by statute of the state. The major advantage to having a corporation is that of *limited liability.* The concept of limited liability simply stated revolves around the fact that the corporation is liable for the debts of the corporation and the shareholders are generally not. In the event that a corporation defaults on its debts, the creditors of that corporation cannot, except under limited circumstances, proceed after the personal assets of the shareholders of a corporation. This concept of limited liability applies to all types of corporate entities, whether they are "C" corporations, "S" corporations, closed corporations, limited liability companies, and so on. Corporations not formed under the laws of a specific state are called *foreign corporations* in that state and in order to transact business in that state, must qualify to do business and receive a certificate of authority to do business.

Closed Corporations: Generally speaking, a closed corporation is a domestic corporation formed in conformance with the requirements of the closed corporation laws of a state. A closed corporation has certain advantages and certain disadvantages with respect to its operation and parties should be advised to seek counsel from their attorney and accountant prior to making the decision to become a closed corporation.

Subchapter "S" Corporations: Subchapter "S" of the Internal Revenue Code provides that a corporation may elect to be treated as a *subchapter "S" corporation*. The essential advantage to the subchapter "S" corporation is that, although it has the limited liability feature of all corporations, gains and losses are passed through to the shareholders, avoiding the two-tiered tax (one at the corporate level and one at the individual level). There are many restrictions to the subchapter "S" corporation. For example, there may not be an excess of shareholders, a corporation may not be a shareholder, a foreign individual may not be a shareholder, there are passive and active loss limitations, restrictions to use of the corporate taxable year, certain limitations on employee benefits which are allowable, and so on.

Limited Liability Companies: The regulations in some states relative to limited liability companies are similar to corporations that have many of the important characteristics of partnerships. Essentially, a limited liability company is a combination of the positive aspects of a "C" corporation, an "S" corporation, and a limited partnership. The owners of limited liability companies have the *limited liability* feature of corporate entities. However, the limited liability company is generally treated as a partnership for federal income tax purposes and, therefore, is taxed much like a subchapter "S" corporation. The limited liability company is different from the subchapter "S" corporation in that it does not have many of the restrictions placed on the subchapter "S" corporation. *Note:* Please check with the laws of each individual state.

Creditor: The person or business to whom a debtor or business owes a debt or obligation.

Debtor: One who owes money; the borrower or mortgagor.

Depreciation: (1) The loss in value due to deterioration through ordinary wear and tear, action of the elements, functional, or economic obsolescence. (2) For income tax purposes, depreciation is an expense deduction taken for the cost in depreciable property. (3) For an asset, the time period over which depreciable cost is to be allocated is called depreciable life. For tax purposes, depreciable life may be shorter than estimated service life.

Disclaimer: A statement denying legal responsibility. Such a statement, however, would not relieve the maker of any liabilities for fraudulent acts or misrepresentations.

Discretionary Cash Flow: Often called discretionary earnings, it is the earnings of a business before deduction for income taxes, nonoperating income and expenses, nonrecurring income and expenses, depreciation, amortization, interest income, interest expense, and total compensation to owner for services which could be provided by a sole owner/manager.

Earnest Money: Down payment made by a purchaser as evidence of good faith.

EBIT: Earnings before interest and taxes.

EBITDA: Earnings before interest, taxes, depreciation, and amortization.

EBT: Earnings before taxes.

Economic Life: The period over which property may be profitably used.

Escrow: The process by which money and/or documents are held by a disinterested third person until the satisfaction of the terms and conditions of the escrow instructions.

Fair Market Value: The amount at which a business would change hands between a willing seller and a willing buyer when neither is acting under compulsion and when both have reasonable knowledge of the relevant facts.

Fiduciary: (1) Noun: A person who is in a position of trust in relation to another party; or a person in a confidential or trust position. (2) Adjective: Confidential, such as a confidential relationship. Fiduciary refers to the relationship of an agent to a principal.

Financial Statement: A formal statement (usually called the balance sheet) of the financial status and net worth of a person or company, setting forth and classifying assets and liabilities as of a specified date in time. For the purposes of marketing businesses, a statement of sales, expenses, and profits (usually called the profit and loss statement) is also included which covers a specific period of time. The date of the balance sheet will need to correspond to the last date of the period of time of the profit and loss statement.

Finder's Fee: Fee paid to another properly licensed professional for locating and introducing a potential client to an intermediary.

Fiscal Year: A business year for tax, corporate, or accounting purposes, as opposed to a calendar year. For example, a commonly used fiscal year is the 12-month period from July 1 through June 30 of the following year.

Franchise: (1) A right or privilege conferred by law, such as a state charter authorizing the formation and existence of corporations. (2) The private contractual right to operate a business using a designated trade name and the operating procedures of a parent company.

Going Concern: (1) The value of an enterprise, or an interest therein, as a going concern. (2) Intangible elements of value in a business enterprise resulting from factors such as having a trained workforce, an operational plant, and the necessary licenses, systems, and procedures in place.

Goodwill: Sometimes called *Blue Sky,* it is the portion of the price of a business which cannot be supported by asset value and/or established valuation methodology. It is the intangible asset that arises as a result of name, reputation, customer patronage, location, products, and similar factors that have not been separately identified and/or valued but which generate economic benefits.

Gross Income: The total income derived from a business before deductions for expenses, depreciation, taxes, and similar allowances.

Holdback: That portion of a loan payment(s) which will not be paid until some additional requirement has been attained.

Intermediary: (1) A professional who normally earns all or the larger portion of his/her income from serving buyers and sellers of businesses. His/her services normally include locating and introducing the parties, providing information and advice, maintaining communications, and coordinating negotiations through the closing process. (2) Intermediaries may come from various disciplines, such as business brokers, accountants, attorneys, business counselors, business consultants, M & A specialists, and so on.

Inventory: An itemized list of property.

Joint Venture: The joining of two or more people in a specific business enterprise.

Lease: An agreement, written or unwritten, transferring the right to exclusive use of real and/or personal property.

Lease Option: A lease containing a clause that gives the tenant the right to purchase a business or property under specified conditions.

Lessee: The person or entity to whom a business or property is rented or leased.

Lessor: The person or entity who rents or leases a business or property.

Letter of Intent: An expression of intent of purchase without creating any firm legal obligation to do so. Letters of Intent may additionally contain definite binding agreements to purchase.

Lien: A charge or claim which one person or entity (lienor) has upon the assets of another person *or entity* (lienee) as security for a debt or obligation.

Line of Credit: Normally, the maximum amount of money a bank will lend one of its more reliable and credit-worthy customers without the need for additional formal loan submissions.

Listing: A written employment agreement between a business owner and an intermediary (also called broker and other terms) authorizing the intermediary to find a buyer or tenant. A listing may take several forms:

> *Sole and Exclusive Right to Sell and Security Agreement:* The broker is given the sole and exclusive right to sell the business during the listing period. Even if the owner should sell to someone procured by the owner, or anyone else, the broker is entitled to a fee. This is most commonly used by successful brokers. Brokers can apply their best efforts, secure in the knowledge that the right to a commission cannot be defeated by anyone during the listing period. Additionally, the owner gives the broker a security interest in the business to secure the payment of the fee.

> *Exclusive Agency Listing:* The owner agrees that a fee for the sale of the business will be payable only to the broker named in the listing agreement and that the business will not be listed or sold by another broker. However, if the business is sold by the owner to a buyer which the owner finds, without the assistance of any broker, then the listing broker is not entitled to a fee.

> *Open Listing:* The owner lists the business with a broker at a specified price, agreeing to pay a fee on that price or any

other price that may be acceptable to the owner. However, the owner retains the right to sell the property personally or to list the property with other brokers. Should the owner give an open listing to a number of brokers, only the broker who is the procuring cause of the sale is entitled to a fee.

Net Listing: A net listing is a contract to find a buyer for the business at a certain net price to the owner. Most states do not encourage net listings.

Other listing agreements exist in many states but are not often used or encouraged.

Market Value: See *Fair Market Value.*

Merger: The uniting or combining of two or more businesses or entities into one.

Net Assets: Total assets less total liabilities.

Net Operating Profit: The mathematical difference between gross profit and total operating expenses. As the name suggests, net operating profit is the profit that results from the normal operations of the business, as distinct from the income or expenses arising from nonoperating sources that may appear on the accountant's income/expense statement that may include income received from and expenses incurred in connection with activities of the business that are outside the scope of normal business operations.

Net Income: Revenues less all expenses, including taxes.

Net Sales: Gross sales, minus sales taxes, returns, and allowances.

Noncompete Agreement: Agreement given by a seller of a business not to compete against the buyer in an agreed area for a specified time.

Nonoperating/Noncontributing Asset: An asset not necessary to the operation of a business or the generation of its revenues.

Note: A document signed by the borrower, stating the loan amount, the interest rate, the time and method of repayment, and the obligation to repay.

Option: An agreement to keep open, over a period of time, an offer to sell.

GLOSSARY

Owner: A generic term used to represent proprietor, general partner, controlling shareholder, or other person controlling ownership of a business.

Owner's Salary: All salary, wages, and payroll expenses paid to the owner.

Owner's Total Compensation: Total owner's salary, benefits, and perks after compensation of all other owners has been adjusted to market value.

Partnerships: Partnerships are governed by the partnership act(s) of individual states. Generally, for income tax purposes, a partnership includes a syndicate, group, pool, joint venture, or other unincorporated organizations, in which more than one individual joins together for a business purpose. A corporation may be a participating partner in a partnership. A partnership agreement defines the share of profits and losses each partner will bear. Each partner must include, on his individual income tax return, his distributive share of each item of gain or loss from the partnership taxable income. Absent provisions in a partnership agreement relative to division of gains or losses, each partnership is governed by the laws of the state. An important feature of partnerships is that each partner is *jointly and severally liable* for the acts of the other partners in the furtherance of partnership business. In essence, this means that all partners share personal liability of the acts of the partnership or each of the partners in the furtherance of the partnership business. The primary tax advantage in forming a partnership is that the partnership as such is not a taxable entity. The individual partners are allowed to deduct the losses of the partnership and are taxed upon the income of the partnership.

> *Limited Partnerships* are defined by the laws of the state and generally act as a partnership formed by two or more persons, having as its members one or more general partners and one or more limited partners. The general partners in a limited partnership have unlimited liability with respect to acts of the partnership or the partners. On the other hand, each limited partner is only liable to the extent of that partner's capital contribution to the partner-

ship. In order to form a limited partnership, a filing is generally required with the secretary of state. Once the filing is completed, a certificate of limited partnership is issued by the secretary of state. This is in contrast to a general partnership, where no filing is generally required to form a partnership, other than with the IRS.

Professional or Personal Service Partnerships are a particular type of partnership that has as its purpose either the practice of a profession or the sale of personal services, as contrasted to the sale of tangible property. A significant factor in the operation of this type of partnership is that the partnership income is produced by personal services and usually there is no need for large amounts of capital. Generally, professional or personal service partnerships are only formed by doctors, lawyers, dentists, and other licensed professionals.

Family Partnerships are one of many other types of partnership arrangements. This class of partnership is generally similar in construction to any other commercial partnership except that the partners are all related by family ties. These partnerships are usually created to distribute income to a wider number of individuals and therefore reduce the tax incidence on a specific individual who has been in a high tax bracket (such as the breadwinner in the family). There are valuable income splitting opportunities in including a taxpayer's children or parents in a family partnership, or in converting a proprietorship into a family partnership.

Personal Property: Generally, all things which are not real property; things of a temporary or movable nature.

Perquisites (Perks): Benefits paid at the discretion of the owner which are not required to operate the business.

Power of Attorney: A written instrument authorizing a person, the attorney-in-fact, to act as an agent on behalf of another to the extent indicated in the instrument.

Practice of Law: Rendering services which are peculiar to the law profession, such as preparing legal documents, giving legal advice and counsel, or construing contracts by which legal rights are secured.

Price: Usually listed or asking price which is the total amount for which a business or ownership interest is offered for sale.

Principal: (1) Any person, partnership, association, or corporation who authorizes or employs another, called the agent, to do certain acts on behalf of the principal. See *Agency.* (2) Also means money or capital, as opposed to interest or income.

Prorate: To divide equally or proportionately, according to time or use.

Real Property: Land; the surface of the earth, and whatever is erected, growing upon, or affixed to the land; including that which is below it and the space above it. Synonymous with land, realty, and real estate.

Recasting: The adjustments to the accountant's income/expense statement which reflect variations in treatment of expenses as they relate to owner's perquisites and to proprietary income for the purpose of arriving at seller's discretionary cash flow.

SDCF: Seller's discretionary cash flow. See Discretionary Cash Flow.

Sole and Exclusive Right to Sell Listing Agreement: A listing whereby the owner of a business appoints one intermediary as sole and exclusive agent for a specified period of time. No matter who sells the business, including the owner, personally, the intermediary is entitled to a commission and/or fee as agreed.

Sole Proprietorship: A method of owning a business in which one person owns the entire business and reports all profits and losses directly on his or her personal income tax return, as contrasted with corporate, joint, or partnership ownership.

Statute of Frauds: State law that requires certain contracts to be in writing and signed by the parties to be charged or held to the agreement in order to be legally enforceable.

Tax-Deferred Exchange: A method of deferring capital gains by exchanging property for other like property.

Title: The right to ownership.

Transaction Value: Total of all consideration passed at any time between buyer and seller for ownership interest in a business, which may include, but not limited to:

Remuneration for tangible and intangible assets, such as:

> Furniture, fixtures, equipment, machinery
> Supplies, inventory
> Cash, working capital
> Noncompetition agreement(s)
> Employment/consultation agreement(s)
> Licenses, patents
> Customer lists
> Franchise agreements
> Franchise fees
> Assumed liabilities
> Stock options
> Stock or stock redemptions
> Real properties, including leases
> Royalties
> Earn outs
> Other future considerations

Triple Net Lease: A net, net, net lease, where in addition to the stipulated rent, the lessee assumes payment of all expenses associated with the operation of the property. This includes both fixed expenses, such as taxes and insurance, and all operating expenses, including costs of maintenance and repair. In some rare cases the triple net tenant even pays the interest payments on the lessor's mortgage on the property.

Uniform Commercial Code: The law which established a unified and comprehensive scheme for the regulation of security transactions in personal property and bulk sales laws.

Variable Interest Rate: An approach to financing in which the lender is permitted to alter the interest rate, with a certain period of advance notice, based upon an agreed basic index.

Venture Capital: Unsecured money directed toward an investment.

Because of the risks involved, it usually commands the highest rate of return for its investment.

Working Capital: The amount by which current assets exceed current liabilities. Liquid assets available for the conduct of daily business.

Wraparound Mortgage: A method of refinancing in which the new mortgage is placed in a secondary or subordinate position.

INDUSTRY RESOURCES*

**ABC Alliance of Business
Consultants**
5869 S. Riviera Court
Aurora, CO 80015
Telephone: 303-627-0685
Fax: 303-627-0684
Contact Person: Bill Bumstead

**Alliance of Business Brokers
and Intermediaries**
1007 Church St., #310
Evanston, IL 60201
Telephone: 847-866-1188
Contact Person: George
Stevenson

**American Arbitration
Association**
1150 Connecticut Ave., NW, 6th
Floor
Washington, DC 20036
Telephone: 202-331-7073
Fax: 202-331-3356

American Business Lists
5711 S. 86th Circle
P. O. Box 27347
Omaha, NE 68127
Telephone: 402-592-9000
Fax: 402-331-1505

**American Institute of Certified
CPAs**
Harborside Financial Center, 201
Plaza III
Jersey City, NJ 07311-3881

American Society of Appraisers
P. O. Box 17265
Washington, DC 20041

**Arizona Association of Business
Brokers, Inc. (AABB)**
6644 E. Paseo San Andres
Tucson, AZ 85710
Telephone: 520-298-0225
Contact Person: Tim Bathen

*Note: You will find additional listings at the end of Chapters 4 and 13.

Association for Corporate Growth
4350 DiPaola Center, Ste. C
Deerlove Road
Glenview, IL 60025
Telephone: 708-699-1331

Association of Independent Certified Public Accountants (AICPA)
1445 Pennsylvania Ave., NW
Washington, DC 20004-1081
Telephone: 202-434-9234

Association of Midwest Business Brokers (AMBB)
1020 West Mallard
Palatine, IL 60067
Telephone: 708-358-9404
Contact Person: Linda Purcell

The Association of New England Business Brokers (NEBBA)
15 Walden Street
Concord MA 01742
Telephone: 508-287-5278
Contact Person: Rocco Pezza

Bisquest
http://www/bizquest.com

BIZCOMPS
P. O. Box 711777
San Diego, CA 92171
Telephone: 619-457-0366
Contact Person: Jack Sanders

Bumstead, William Erik, LPI
Worldwide Claim Services, Inc.
9400 N. Central Expressway #420
Dallas, TX 75231
Telephone: 214-899-7281

Fax: 214-369-8314
E-mail: FindFraud@aol.com

Business Brokerage Press
P.O. Box 247
Concord, MA 01742
Telephone: 508-369-5254
Fax: 508-371-1156
Contact Person: Tom West

Business Brokers Associates of Southern California (BBASC)
15431 Runnymede St.
Van Nuys, CA 91406
Telephone: 818-994-0216
Contact Person: Stanley Gold

Business Brokers Association of San Diego
3111 Camino Del Rio N. #400
San Diego, CA 92108
Telephone: 619-528-2222
Contact Person: Jim Pagni

Business Broker Web
http://www.business-broker.com

Business Evaluation Systems
P. O. Box 1262
Dickinson, TX 77539
Telephone: 713-337-3508
Contact Person: George Abraham

Business Opportunities Web Page
http://www.suzton.com/opportunity.html

Business Opportunity Council of California (B.O.C.C.)
355 S. Grand Ave. #2550
Los Angeles, CA 90071
Telephone: 213-437-4006
Contact Person: Chris Paris

Business Opportunity Mall
http://webmall.clever.net/
    infohwy.htm

Business Resource Group
http://www.indirect.com/www/
    gstarman/brgprof.html

Bus-Net
http://www.busopps.com

**California Association of
    Business Brokers**
1608 W. Campbell Ave.
Campbell, CA 95008
Telephone: 408-379-7748
Contact Person: Ron Johnson

Clari Mergers
http://www.clari.biz.mergers

**Coalition of Small and
    Independent Business
    Associations**
200 Tower City Center
Cleveland, OH 44113
Telephone: 216-621-3300

Colorado Society of CPAs
7979 E. Tufts, Ste. 500
Denver, CO 80237

Cooper, Gary, CPA
Cooper and Associates
9400 N. Central Expressway,
    Suite 420
Dallas, TX 75231
Telephone: 214-369-5820
Fax: 214-265-9376

Data Base America
100 Paragon Dr. S.
Montvale, NJ 07645
Telephone: 800-223-7777
Fax: 201-476-2300

The Entrepreneur Link
http://www.lainet.com/thelink

**Environmental Protection
    Agency (EPA)**
Call for Regional Offices: 800-
    535-0202

**Financial Intelligence Network
    (FINET)**
9134 Union Cemetery Rd. #413
Cincinnati, OH 45249
Telephone: 513-459-9531
Contact Person: Natalie Price

**Florida Business Brokers
    Association (FBBA)**
8120 W. Oakland Park Blvd.,
    2nd floor
Sunrise, FL 33351
Telephone: 954-749-2334
Contact Person: Peter Louis

Franchise Brokers Network
3617 A. Silverside Rd.
Wilmington, DE 19810
Telephone: 302-478-0200
Fax: 302-478-9217

Franchise Solutions
P. O. Box 5178
Portsmouth, NH 03802-5178
Telephone: 800-898-4455
Fax: 603-430-2942
http://www.bluefin-net/"fransale

**Georgia Association of Business
    Brokers (GABB)**
303 Covey Court
Woodstock, GA 30188
Telephone: 770-442-1608

Immigration and Visas to the USA
American Advisory Press
28100 US 19 North, Suite 502
Clearwater, FL 34621
Telephone: 800-844-9855
Fax: 813-796-2953
Contact Person: Ramon Carrion

Institute of Business Appraisers
P. O. Box 1447
Boynton Beach, FL 33435

InterAd (WA Group)
http://www.nia.com/bus_opp/

The International Franchise Association
1350 New York Ave., NW, Suite 900
Washington, DC 20005-4709
Telephone: 202-628-8000
Fax: 202-628-0812

International Merger and Acquisition Professionals (IMAP)
60 Revere Dr. Ste. 500
Northbrook, IL 60062
Telephone: 708-480-9037

Investigative Due-Diligence
Bumstead, William Erik, LPI
420 Glen Lakes Tower
9400 North Central Expy.
Dallas, TX 75231
Telephone: 972-396-9746
Fax: 214-369-8314

Jeff Jones, FCBI, BCB
Business Brokerage and Appraisal Services
10301 Northwest Fwy. #200
Houston, TX 77092
Telephone: 713-680-1200
Fax: 713-680-8300

The Loop
http://www.loopnet.com

M&A Marketplace
http://mktplc.com/cfnet

M&A On Line
http://www.maol.com/maol/

M&A Source
(International Business Brokers Association)
11250 Roger Bacon Dr. Suite 8
Reston, VA 20090
Telephone: 703-437-4377

Marketplace Information Corporation
Dun & Bradstreet
460 Totten Pond Rd. Ste. 30
Waltham, MA 02154
Telephone: 800-967-4646

Michigan Business Brokers Association, West Chapter (MBBA-West)
P. O. Box 7
Freeport, MI 49325
Telephone: 616-945-5874

The Money Store
Telephone: 800-722-3066

National Association for the Self-Employed (NASE)
2121 Precinct Line Road
Hurst, TX 76054
Telephone: 800-232-NASE

National Association of Certified Valuation Analysts
1245 E. Brickyard Rd., #110
Salt Lake City, UT 84106

National Association of Enrolled Agents (NAEA)
200 Orchard Ridge Drive #302
Gaithersburg, MD 20878
Telephone 301-212-9608
Contact Person: Jim Jilek

National Association of Women Business Owners (NAWBO)
1413 K. Street NW
Washington DC 20005
Telephone: 301-608-2590

National Business Exchange
http/www.nbe.com

National Federation of Independent Businesses (NFIB)
Capital Gallery East Suite 700
600 Maryland Ave. SW
Washington, DC 20024
Telephone 202-573-2385

National Minority Business Council (NMBC)
235 E. 42nd St.
New York, NY 10017
Telephone: 212-573-2385

National Society of Accountants (NSA)
1010 North Fairfax Street
Alexandria, VA 22314
Telephone: 703-549-6400

National Society of Tax Professionals (NSTP)
P. O. Box 2575
Vancouver, WA 98668
Telephone: 206-695-8309

New York Association of Business Brokers (NYABB)
111 Grant Ave.
Endicott, NY 13760
Telephone: 607-754-5990
Contact Person: Herb Cohen

Northwest Association of Business Brokers (NABB)
P. O. Box 21305
Seattle, WA 98111
Telephone: 206-624-NABB
Contact Person: Curtis Casp

Ohio Business Brokers Association
1515 Bethel Road
Columbus, OH 43220
Telephone: 614-451-5100
Contact Person: Dave Goll

Padgett Business Services
160 Hawthorne Park
Athens, GA 30606
Telephone: 706-548-1040
Contact Person: Roger Harris

Riggs/Allen Report
P. O. Box 795
Southport, CT 06490
Telephone: 203-254-2991
Fax: 203-254-8452

R. L. Polk & Co.
Telephone: 810-728-7000

SCORE (Service Corps of Retired Executives)
409 3rd St. SW, 4th Floor
Washington, DC 20024

Small Business Administration
Telephone: 800-827-5722
Fax: 202-205-7701

Small Business Development Centers (SBDC)
Telephone: 402-595-2387

Small Business Survival Committee
Ms. Karen Kerrigan, President
1320 18th St. NW, #200
Washington, DC 20036

Texas Association of Business Brokers (TABB)
P. O. Box 820398
Dallas, TX 75382-0398
Telephone: 214-373-1560
Fax: 214-373-1560

U.S. Chamber of Commerce
1615 H Street NW
Washington, DC 20062-2000
Telephone: 202-463-5604
Contact Person: David K. Voight

U.S. Small Business Administration (SBA)
Washington, DC 20416

Washington (DC) Council of Professional Business Brokers, Inc. (WBBA)
800 17th St. NW
Washington, DC 20006
Telephone: 202-223-9669
Contact Person: Richard Dodson

World M&A Network
717 D St. NW, #300
Washington, DC 20004-2807
Telephone: 202-628-6900
Contact Person: John Bailey
http://www.cqi.com/MandA/index.html

Venture Connect
http://www.vencon.com

BIBLIOGRAPHY

Abraham, George D. *Business Evaluation Systems National Data Base.* Dickinson, TX, 1996.

———— . *Business Evaluation Systems Software.* New York: John Wiley & Sons, Inc., 1997.

American Society of Appraisers, *Business Valuation Review.* Updated monthly.

Bumstead, William W. *Basic Business Brokerage.* Houston, TX: Business Exchange Network, 1994.

———— . *52 Steps to Find Buyers and Sellers of Businesses.* Reston, VA: International Business Brokers Association, 1996.

———— . *How to Sell Business Valuations.* Reston, VA: International Business Brokers Association, 1997.

————. *Principles and Ethics of Business Brokerage.* Dallas, TX: Texas Association of Business Brokers, 1995.

———— . *Professional Priority Planning.* Houston, TX: Achievers International, 1993.

Business Valuation Update. Willamette Management Associates. Updated monthly.

Country Business Services. *Small Business Acquisition Manual.* 1981.

Desmond, Glenn, and Richard Kelly. *Business Valuation Handbook.* Llano, CA: Valuation Press, Inc., 1977.

BIBLIOGRAPHY

Financial Research Associates. *Financial Studies of the Small Business.* Updated annually.

Hanson, James M. *Guide to Buying or Selling a Business.* Mercer Island, Washington: 1979.

Jones, Jeff. *Handbook of Business Valuation.* New York: John Wiley & Sons, Inc., 1992.

———. *Handbook of Buying and Selling Small and Mid-Size Companies.* New York: John Wiley & Sons, Inc., 1996.

Jurek, Walter. *A Reference Manual of Practical Information on Buying or Selling a Business.* Stow, Ohio: Quality Services, Inc., 1976.

Kohl, John C., and Atlee M. Kohl. *The Smart Way to Buy a Business.* Irving, TX: Woodland Publishers, 1986.

Meigs, Walter B. and Robert F. Meigs. *Financial Accounting,* Third Edition, 1993.

Miles, Raymond C. *Basic Business Appraisal.* New York: John Wiley & Sons, Inc., 1984.

Pratt, Shannon P. *Valuing a Business*, Third Edition. Homewood, IL: Dow Jones–Irwin, 1996.

———. *Valuing a Business*, Second Edition. Homewood, IL: Dow Jones–Irwin, 1989.

———. *Valuing a Business.* Homewood, IL: Dow Jones–Irwin, 1981.

Revenue Ruling 59–60. Internal Revenue Service, 26 CFR 20.2031-2: Valuation of Stocks and Bonds. 1959.

Sanders, Jack. *BizComps.* San Diego, CA. 1997.

Shannon Moris Associates. *Annual Statement Studies.* Updated annually.

Standard and Poors Industry Surveys. Updated annually.

Tetrualt, Wilfred F. *Buying and Selling Business Opportunities.* New York: Addison-Wesley, 1979.

U.S. Global Trade Outlook. Washington, DC: U.S. Department of Commerce. Updated annually.

U.S. Small Business Administration. *Annual Report.* Washington,

DC: United States Small Business Administration. Updated annually.

ValuSource. *Cash Flow Forecasting*. New York: John Wiley & Sons, Inc., 1996. Updated annually.

ValuSource. *Fixed Asset Analyzer*. New York: John Wiley & Sons, Inc., 1996. Updated annually.

ValuSource. *IRS Corporate Ratios*. New York: John Wiley & Sons, Inc., 1996. Updated annually.

ValuSource. *1997 Mid-Market Comparables*. New York: John Wiley & Sons, Inc., 1997.

Wall Street Journal

INDEX

INDEX

INDEX